The Warrior Princess

The WARRIOR PRINCESS

Book III of Edmund Spenser's *The Faerie Queene*

Updated and annotated by

Roy Maynard

canonpress
Moscow, Idaho

Published by Canon Press
P.O. Box 8729, Moscow, ID 83843
800–488–2034 | www.canonpress.com

Roy Maynard, *The Warrior Princess:* Edmund Spenser's *The Faerie Queene,* Book III.
Copyright © 2018 by Roy Maynard.

Cover design by Rachel Hoffmann.
Cover image from "Britomart," a watercolor by Walter Crane (1900).
Interior layout by Laura Storm.
Printed in the United States of America.

All rights reserved. No part of this publication may be reproduced, stored in a retrieval system, or transmitted in any form by any means, electronic, mechanical, photocopy, recording, or otherwise, without prior permission of the author, except as provided by USA copyright law.

Library of Congress Cataloging-in-Publication Data
Spenser, Edmund, 1552?-1599.
 [Faerie queene. Book 3]
The warrior princess : Edmund Spenser's The faerie queene, book III / [Edmund Spenser] ; updated and annotated by Roy Maynard.
   p. cm.
ISBN 978-1-59128-095-8
 1. Knights and knighthood—Poetry. 2. Virtues—Poetry. 3. Spenser, Edmund, 1552?–1599. Faerie queene. I. Maynard, Roy. II. Title.
PR2358.A3 2013
821'.3--dc23

2011029357

18 19 20 21 22 23 24   9 8 7 6 5 4 3 2 1

*To my daughters, Laurel and Blythe:
May you make your ways fearlessly
with God's purity and strength.*

Contents

INTRODUCTION 1

PREFACE 5

CANTO I 7
   Word Play and Discussion Questions 28

CANTO II 29
   Edmund Spenser, the Prince of Poets 37
   Word Play and Discussion Questions 47

CANTO III 49
   Word Play and Discussion Questions 69

CANTO IV 71
   Chastity 81
   Word Play and Discussion Questions 91

CANTO V 93
   Word Play and Discussion Questions 111

CANTO VI 113
   King Arthur 125
   Word Play and Discussion Questions 133

CANTO VII 135
   Word Play and Discussion Questions 155

CANTO VIII 157
   Merlin 166
   Word Play and Discussion Questions 175

CANTO IX 177
   Word Play and Discussion Questions............. 195

CANTO X 197
   Amazons 204
   Word Play and Discussion Questions............. 217

CANTO XI 219
   Word Play and Discussion Questions.............237

CANTO XII............................. 239
   Love....................................250
   Word Play and Discussion Questions.............254

INTRODUCTION

Edmund Spenser's tomb at Westminster Abbey has the inscription, "The Prince of Poets." Leaving aside Homer, Virgil, and the Ramones for the moment, we could have a lively debate on whom that makes the "king." But Spenser was one of the greats. If you've read Books I and II of his unfinished English epic, *The Faerie Queene,* you know that by now.

A devout Christian, he was primarily concerned with what we would now call "preaching to the choir," but not in a bad way. He focused on the sanctification of Christians, rather than evangelism of non-Christians.

In my view, his concern seemed to be that the English Reformation (conceived in Henry VIII's vanity and confirmed in the blood of his innocent wives) would set aside virtue, as Henry had done, in favor of political gain. Spenser wrote of a Christianity many of us would recognize. It was based upon biblical concepts such as the fall of man and the need for grace (even for kings), and it dealt with tough issues, such as temptation, "apostasy" (backsliding), lust, and even sex.

He wrote for adults. I'd have to give Book III a PG rating (in some parts, PG-13), because there are portions unsuitable for children. Yet this edition is no "adaptation" for the young, like the Charles and Mary Lamb book on the "Stories of Shakespeare." You'll get the real thing here—lust, sexual innuendos, and torture, among other things. There are portions that might (should) make you blush. Yet that was Spenser's intent. No one can accuse this guy of overlooking sin when it should have been pointed out and condemned.

Spenser was a contemporary of Shakespeare but gets far less attention these days. Part of the reason is he wrote in what was, even at the time, archaic language (old words, tough to follow even for the few literate people of the day), and he mixed allegory with preachiness (the word I'd use is didacticism).

But he also did some pretty good storytelling. I've always said Book I of *The Faerie Queene* is basically *Star Wars: A New Hope,* but cooler. (You have your farm boy, your distressed princess, your betrayals, even your magical sword, though Luke's was called a "lightsaber"; and Spenser has a monster that barfs on its victims, which George Lucas didn't.)

Yet while Spenser's language might seem out of touch with the times, Spenser himself wasn't. He saw his queen (Elizabeth I, the daughter of Henry VIII) for what she was: both a symbol (a replacement in the hearts of the people for the Virgin Mary they left behind with Catholicism) and a fallen human being. I think that's one reason we never actually meet her character—her avatar, if you will, Glorianna—in the text of the poem. His letter about the epic mentions her and gives some back-story, but she never actually shows up in his poem.

As Douglas Brooks-Davies of the University of Manchester wrote in his 1996 updated edition's introduction to the poem, "He dedicated it to an empress. But in his daily life he saw (and, if he is a poet worth reading, he sympathized profoundly with) the wretched state of those over which she ruled."[1]

Brooks-Davies goes on to discuss her purported virginity but also her fury at those of her "favorites" in her court who went and got married (Leicester, Raleigh). Elizabeth was no saint, and Spenser knew it.

But like any sub-creator, to borrow a concept from Tolkien, Spenser had some say-so over the world he was fashioning. As Brooks-Davies points out, he wrote about how things ought to be, not necessarily how they were.

Who can blame him? Spenser's England was a country in the midst of religious and political turmoil. The Reformation had not yet taken a firm hold nor had it fully found its theological feet. There were dragons of all kinds in his England: theological, philosophical, and moral—not to mention the international threats and internal political instability. Spenser's role, as he saw it, was to help ground the new faith in the hearts of the English.

One thing that draws me to Book III of *The Faerie Queene* is the main character, Britomart (her name is a combination of Britania and of Mars or Martial, indicating war). Elizabeth was a wartime queen; she faced the Spanish Armada, among many other threats. Spenser saw the strength women were truly capable of. While I wouldn't call him a sixteenth-century feminist, I would commend him for recognizing that female characters can be strong and still remain women. For most of the book, Britomart is disguised as a knight-errant, and only a few learn her secret before it's too late and they're looking up at her sword or lance-point.

This fascinates me because I have two daughters myself. Even if no publisher was involved, I think this project would be worthwhile as something to pass on to them as they get older and find themselves assailed by a culture that glorifies

---

1. Douglas Brooks-Davies, *The Fairy Queen by Edmund Spenser* (London: Everyman Classics, 1987 and 1996).

sex. Strength of character, such as that displayed by Britomart, is the only safe way to confront the next few years for them. I hope they benefit from her example.

I'll repeat a few notes I included in the introduction of my update of Book I.

First, don't panic. Yes, at first, reading Spenser may feel as if you're hitchhiking through an entirely different galaxy (particularly Spenser's intro, in which he expands his praise of Elizabeth beyond the improbable).[2]

Spenser is actually doing this on purpose (just as Charles Dickens, though desperately in need of a decent editor with a "delete" button, wrote really long novels because he was paid by the word). Spenser's goal was to create a classical- and medieval-style epic for England. So he had to obey the rules. Those included using iambic pentameter (which he was pretty good at). He also used *amplificatio* (ways of amplifying or expanding his poem), such as *expolitio* (conveying the same thought in a number of different ways), *circumlocutio* (not calling things and people by their direct names), *ornatus* (switching around the order of words), and *diversio* (breaking off in the middle of an exciting part to talk about something completely different—a way of building suspense).

Now, I will confess that I've taken greater liberties with Spenser's language and word-choices than I did in *Fierce Wars and Faithful Loves* (Book I). That's on purpose; Spenser seems to have become more complicated as he went along. And he *made up words*. Apparently, spelling hadn't been invented yet, because he would spell the same word (with the same meaning) several different ways. For example, in meaning "dwelling place," he used the words *won, wone,* and *wonne.*

And what was it with all the extra *e*'s? Those English writers tacked extra ones onto any word they could. History, of course, tells us that eventually even *they* had had enough of "faire" and "ye olde shoppe" and such, and packed all of the extra *e*'s into crates and shipped them to America—whereupon, naturally, we dressed up like Indians and chucked them into Boston Harbor.

But trust me. You'll be surprised at how quickly you catch on and become more comfortable with Spenser's little ways.

Another recommendation is to read it aloud. The ear can unravel things the eye often can't; just listen to an average conversation with its incomplete sentences, "ums," interruptions, and *non sequiturs,* and tell me it would be easier to understand if it were written down.

---

2. If you caught the references to Douglas Adams' *The Hitchhiker's Guide to the Galaxy* (before you looked down here), you get an extra five points on the first quiz. Tell your teacher I said so. Plus, it means you're ready for Spenser.

But above all, don't give up. Give him a few cantos (chapters) to win you over before you abandon the book. This isn't easy reading, but its rewards are worth the effort.

I have chosen to include Spenser's brief introductory verses in their original language, just so you get a taste of Spenser's English; they're merely the mandatory salute to his queen and patron, Elizabeth I, and calling on the muses to aid him.[3]

Don't think of this as a chore; think of it as a day or two with a fine fairy tale. And as G. K. Chesterton knew, fairy tales are a necessity of life: "Fairy tales are more than true; not because they tell us that dragons exist, but because they tell us that dragons can be beaten."

Roy Maynard
May 2011

---

3. A note on the meter: each paragraph or "stanza" contains nine lines, with eight of those lines in iambic pentameter, and a single line of iambic hexameter. The rhyme scheme is ababbcbcc, which means that though the rhyming goes back and forth, we end with two rhyming lines, with the last one being extra long, which helps the somewhat strung-out stanzas make a clean landing. It is so unique to him that it is called the "Spenserian stanza." Despite how drawn out such a form is and how much rhyming it forced Spenser to do (and as you will see he sometimes modified the spelling of words to force a rhyme), it worked well enough that subsequent poets such as Keats have used it as well.

THE THIRD BOOKE OF THE FAERIE QVEENE.

Contayning

THE LEGEND BRITOMARTIS.

or

OF CHASTITY.

It falles me here to write of Chastity[1],
That fairest vertue, farre aboue the rest;
For which what needs me fetch from Faery
Forreine° ensamples,° it to haue exprest?   *foreign / examples*
Sith it is shrined° in my Soueraines° brest,[2]   *enshrined, preserved / Sovereign's*
And form'd so liuely° in each perfect part   *lively*
That to all Ladies, which haue it profest,
Need but behold the pourtraict of her hart,
If pourtrayd it might be by any liuing art.

But liuing art may not least part expresse,
Nor life-resembling pencill it can paint,
All were it Zeuxis or Praxiteles:[3]
His daedale hand would faile, and greatly faint,
And her perfections with his error taint:
Ne° Poets wit, that passeth Painter farre   *nor*
In picturing the parts of beautie daint,
So hard a workmanship aduenture darre,
For fear through want of words her excellence to marre.°   *deface*

---

1. As with previous Canon Press modernizations, we have included the preface in the original spelling.
2. It would be ridiculous for Spenser to begin a book about Chastity without praising Queen Elizabeth, one of the most famous virgins in all history.
3. Zeuxis and Praxiteles were famous Greek sculptors. Even they could not represent chastity with all their skill.

How then shall I, Apprentice of the skill,
That whylome° in diuinest° wits did raine,°   *formerly / diuinest / reign*
Presume so high to stretch mine humble quill?
Yet now my lucklesse lot doth me constraine
Hereto° perforce. But ô dred° Soueraine°   *to this / great / sovereign*
Thus farre forth pardon, sith that choicest° wit   *best*
Cannot your glorious pourtraict° figure plaine   *portrait*
That I in colourd showes may shadow it,
And antique praises vnto° present persons fit.   *unto*

But if in liuing° colours, and right hew,°   *living / hue*
Your selfe you couet° to see pictured,   *covet*
Who can it doe more liuely, or more trew,°   *true*
Then that sweet verse, with Nectar sprinckeled,°   *sprinkled*
In which a gracious seruant° pictured   *servant*
His Cynthia, his heauens° fairest light?[4]   *heaven's*
That with his melting sweetnesse rauished,°   *ravished*
And with the wonder of her beames bright,
My senses lulled are in slomber° of delight.   *slumber*

But let that same delitious° Poet lend   *delicious, pleasing*
A little leaue° vnto a rusticke Muse   *leave*
To sing his mistresse° prayse, and let him mend,   *mistress's*
Ne° let his fairest Cynthia refuse,   *nor*
In mirrours° more then one her selfe to see,   *mirrors*
But either Gloriana let her chuse,°   *choose*
Or in Belphoebe fashioned to bee:
In th'one her rule, in th'other her rare chastitee.[5]

---

4. Spenser is going to use the same verse utilized by Sir Walter Raleigh in his poem to Elizabeth, whom he called Cynthia (Diana, goddess of Virginity).
5. While Raleigh praised Elizabeth as Cynthia, Spenser will praise her by reflecting her in the virtues of Gloriana, the Faerie Queene, and in Belphoebe, another virgin warrior maiden. These characters are Elizabeth's reflections or "mirrours."

Canto I.

Guyon encounters Britomart,
Fair Florimell is chased:
Duessa's trains° and Malecasta's   *plans*
Champions are defaced.°   *defeated*

1

The famous Briton Prince and Faery[1] knight,
After long ways and perilous pains endured,
Having their weary limbs to perfect plight°   *put right, healed*
Restored, and sore wounds right well cured,
Of° the fair Alma[2] greatly were procured,°   *by / pleaded with*
To make there longer sojourn and abode;
But when thereto they might not be allured,°   *persuaded*
From seeking praise, and deeds of arms abroad,
They courteous leave took, and forth together yode.°   *rode forth*

2

But the captived Acrasia° he sent,   *a villainess of Book II*
Because of travel long, a nigher° way,   *nearer*
With a strong guard, all rescue to prevent,[3]
And her to Faerie court safe to convey,
That her for witness of his hard assay,°   *trial*
Unto his Faerie Queene he might present:[4]
But he himself betook another way,

---

1. Whatever you do, don't think of "fairy" in terms of Walt Disney characters or pretty little winged things. In Spenser's world, fairies are more synonymous with the elves of Tolkien's Middle Earth. You don't want to mess with these guys. By the way, these are our old friends, Arthur and Guyon, described as faery because they are knights of Gloriana, the Fairy Queen.
2. Alma is a woman who helps feed, help, and restore battered knights. See Book II, Cantos IX-XI.
3. They wished to prevent her rescue since she still has allies.
4. He sent her to Glorianna to be judged.

To make more trial of his hardiment,[5]
And seek adventures, as he with Prince Arthur went.

3

Long so they traveled through wasteful ways°   *wilderness*
Where dangers dwelt, and perils most did wone,°   *dwell*
To hunt for glory and renowned praise;
Full many countries they did overrun[6]
From the uprising to the setting sun,
And many hard adventures did achieve;
Of all the which they honor ever won,
Seeking the weak oppressed to relieve,
And to recover right for such, as wrong did grieve.

4

At last as through an open plain they yode,°   *rode forth*
They spied a knight, that towards pricked° fair,   *spurred*
And him beside an aged Squire there rode,
That seemed to couch under his shield three-square,
As if that age bade him that burden spare,[7]
And yield it those, that stouter could it wield:
He them espying, began himself prepare,
And on his arm address his goodly shield
That bore a lion passant in a golden field.[8]

5

Which seeing good Sir Guyon, dear besought
The Prince of grace,[9] to let him run that turn.
He granted: then the Faery° quickly raught°   *Guyon / grabbed*
His poignant° spear, and sharply began to spurn   *piercing*
His foamy steed, whose fiery feet did burn
The verdant° grass, as he thereon did tread;   *green*
Not did the other back his foot return,

---

5. That's what knights did; they looked for hard tasks.
6. Sounds a little extreme to me.
7. It appeared too heavy for him (he was old).
8. This is an important detail. A "lion passant" is a lion walking (in this case, on a gold background). It symbolizes strength (obviously), bravery, and, above all, royalty.
9. As a favor, Arthur let Guyon take this challenge.

But fiercely forward came without dread,
And bent his dreadful spear against the other's head.

6

They been met, and both their points arrived,
But Guyon drove so furious and fell,
That seemed both shield and plate it would have rived;°   *splintered*
Nevertheless, it bore his foe not from his saddle,
But made him stagger, as he were not well:
But Guyon self, ere well he was aware,
Nigh a spear's length behind his crupper° fell,   *the rear end of a horse*
Yet in his fall so well himself he bare,
That mischievous mischance his life and limbs did spare.[10]

7

Great shame and sorrow of that fall he took;°   *he was embarrassed*
For never yet, since warlike arms he bore,
And shivering spear in bloody field first shook,
He found himself dishonored so sore.°   *seriously*
Ah gentlest knight, that ever armor bore,
Let not thee grieve dismounted to have been,
And brought to ground, that never wast before;
For not thy fault, but secret power unseen,
That spear enchanted was, which laid thee on the green.

8

But ween[11] thou what wight° thee overthrew,   *creature*
Much greater grief and shamefuller regret
For thy hard fortune than thou wouldst renew,
That of a single damsel[12] thou had met
On equal plain, and there so hard beset;
Even the famous Britomart it was,
Whom strange adventure did from Britain fetch,°   *arrive*
To seek her lover (love far sought alas),
Whose image she had seen in Venus' looking glass.°   *Venus, goddess of love*

---

10. He landed well and did not hurt himself.
11. Some words and their variations are common in Spenser. *Ween, wot,* and *wit* all mean "to know" or "to realize."
12. Hah! It was a girl!

9

Full of disdainful wrath, he fierce uprose,
For to revenge that foul reprochful shame,
And snatching his bright sword began to close° *catch up*
With her on foot, and stoutly forward came;
Die rather would he, then endure that same.
Which when his Palmer[13] saw, he began to fear
His toward° peril and untoward blame, *upcoming*
Which by that new encounter he should rear:° *experience*
For death sat on the point of that enchanted spear.

10

And hasting towards him began fair persuade,
Not to provoke misfortune, nor to believe,
His spear's fault to mend° with cruel blade; *lose to*
For by his mighty science he had seen
The secret virtue of that weapon keen,° *sharp*
That mortal puissance[14] might not withstood:
Nothing on earth might always happy[15] been.
Great hazard were it, and adventure foolhardy,
To lose long gotten honor with one evil hand.° *deed*

11

By such good means he him discouraged,
From prosecuting his revenging rage;
And eke° the Prince like treaty handeled,° *also / persuaded*
His wrathful will with reason to assuage,° *diminish*
And laid the blame, not to his carriage,° *abilities*
But to his starting steed, that swerved aside,
And to the ill purveyance of his page,
That had his furnitures° not firmly tied: *saddle, armor*
So is his angry courage fairly pacified.

12

Thus reconcilement was between them knit,
Through goodly temperance, and affection chaste,

---

13. Guyon has a Palmer or a holy man as his sidekick (see Bk. II, Canto I).
14. *Puissance* meant strength, power, or might. It's one of Spenser's favorite words, so be looking for it.
15. In this case, he means "lucky."

And either vowed with all their power and wit,
To let not others' honor be defaced,
Of friend or foe, whoever it debased,
Nor arms to bear against the other's side:
In which accord the Prince was also placed,
And with that golden chain of concord tied.
So goodly all agreed, they forth aside did ride.

13

O goodly usage° of those antique times,   *tradition*
In which the sword was servant unto right;[16]
When not for malice and contentious crimes,
But all for praise, and proof of manly might,
The martial° brood accustomed to fight: *warlike*
Then honor was the meed° of victory,   *reward*
And yet the vanquished had no despite:°   *abuse*
Let later age that noble use envy,
Vile rancor to avoid, and cruel presumption.

14

Long they thus traveled in friendly ways,
Through countries waste,° and also well edified,°   *desolate / developed*
Seeking adventures hard, to exercise
Their puissance, whilome° full sternly tried: *at times*
At length they came into a forest wide,
Whose hideous horror and sad trembling sound
Full grisly seemed: therein they long did ride,
Yet tract of living creatures none they found,
Save bears, lions, and bulls, which roamed them around.

15

All suddenly out of the thickest brush,
Upon a milk-white palfrey° all alone,   *gentle lady's horse*
A goodly lady did by them rush,
Whose face did seem as clear as crystal stone,
And eke° through fear as white as whale's bone: *also*

---

16. If you forget the whole Goths and Vandals thing. But Spenser is being poetical: in the good old days, being a knight meant something.

Her garments all were wrought of beaten gold,
And all her steed with tinsel trappings shone,
Which fled so fast, that nothing might him° hold,   *the horse*
And scarce them time gave, her passing to behold.[17]

16

Still as she fled, her eye she backward threw,
As fearing evil, that pursued her fast;
And her fair yellow locks behind her flew,
Loosely dispersed with puff of every blast: [18]
All as a blazing star doth far outcast
His hairy bulk, and flaming locks wide-spread,
At sight whereof the people stand aghast:
But the sage wizard° tells, as he has read,   *wise man*
That it implies death and doleful dreariness.

17

So as they gazed after her a while,
Lo where a grisly forester[19] forth did rush,
Breathing out beastly lust her to defile:
His tiring jade° he fiercely forth did push,   *horse*
Through thick and thin, both over bank and bush
In hope her to attain by hook or crook,
That from his gory sides the blood did gush:
Large were his limbs, and terrible his look,
And in his clownish[20] hand a sharp bore spear he shook.

18

Which outrage when those gentle knights did see,
Full of great envy and fell° jealousy,   *great*
They stayed not to advise who first should be,
But all spurred after fast, as they might fly,
To rescue her from shameful villainy.
The Prince and Guyon equally believe

---

17. Seriously, guys, a beautiful woman comes running out of the forest on a horse? Does this happen every day? Do we really want to trust this situation? Think about it.
18. Windblown hair. Another sign. Think about this.
19. One who lives in the forest, often an outlaw.
20. In this case, it means "peasant."

Herself pursued, in hope to win thereby
Most goodly meed,° the fairest dame alive: *reward*
But after the foul forester Timias did strive.

19

The whiles fair Britomart, whose constant° mind, *unchanging*
Would not so lightly follow beauty's[21] chase,
Nor reckoning of lady's love, did stay behind,
And them awaited there a certain space,
To weet° if they would turn back to that place: *know*
But when she saw them gone, she forward went,
As lay her journey, through that perilous pace,
With steadfast courage and stout hardihood;
Nor evil thing she feared, nor evil thing she meant.

20

At last as nigh out of the wood she came,
A stately castle far away she spied,
To which her steps directly she did frame.
That castle was most goodly edified,° *strenghtened*
And placed for pleasure near that forest side:
But fair before the gate a spacious plain,
Mantled with green, itself did spread wide,
On which she saw six knights, that did arraign° *attack*
Fierce battle against one, with cruel might and main.° *force*

21

Mainly° they all at once upon him laid, *with great force*
And sore beset on every side around,
That soon he breathless grew, yet not dismayed,
Nor ever to them yielded foot of ground
All had he lost much blood through many a wound,
But stoutly dealt his blows, and every way
To which he turned in his wrathful strike,
Made them recoil, and fly from dread contempt,
That none of all the six before, him dared to attempt.

21. Now, which is the smarter of the three? From here on out, we are going to go with Britomart rather than with Guyon or Arthur!

22

Like dastard curs,° that having at a bay   *hounds*
The savage beast closed in, in weary chase,
Dare not adventure on the stubborn prey,
Nor bite before, but roam from place to place,
To get a snatch, when turned is his face.
In such distress and doubtful jeopardy,
When Britomart him saw, she ran a pace
Unto his rescue, and with earnest cry,
Bad° those same six forbear that single enemy.   *commanded*

23

But to her cry they would not lend an ear,
Nor ought the more their mighty strokes to cease,
But gathering him round about more near,
Their direful rancor rather did increase;
Until that she rushing through the thickest press,
By force dispersed their compacted group,
And soon compelled to listen unto peace:
Though began she mildly of them to enquire
The cause of their dissension and outrageous ire.

24

Whereto that single knight did answer to the same;
"These six would me force by odds of might,
To change my beloved, and love another dame,[22]
That death me better was, then such a plight,
So unto wrong to yield my wrested right:
For I love one, the truest one on ground,
Nor wish me change; she the Errant Damsel hight,°   *known as*
For whose dear sake full many a bitter stand,
I have endured, and tasted many a bloody wound."

25

"Certainly," said she, "then be ye six to blame,
To weene° your wrong by force to justify: *to teach*
For knight to leave his lady were great shame,

---

22. Force him to foreswear the woman he loves (Una), in favor of another woman.

That faithful is, and better were to die.
All loss is less, and less the infamy,
Than loss of love to him, that loves but one;
Nor may love be compelled by mastery;
For soon as mastery comes, sweet love shall
Take his nimble wings, and soon away is gone."

26

Then spoke one of those six, "There dwells here
Within this castle wall a lady fair,
Whose sovereign beauty hath no living peer,
Thereto so bounteous and so debonair,
That never any might with her compare.
She hath ordained this law, which we approve,
That every knight, which doth this way arrive,
In case he have no lady, nor no love,
Shall do unto her service never to remove.

27

"But if he have a lady or a love,
Then must he her forgo with foul disdain,
Or else with us by dint° of sword approve   *blows, dents*
That she is fairer than our fairest dame,
As did this knight, before ye hither came."
"Indeed," said Britomart, "the choice is hard:
But what reward had he, that overcame?"
"He should advanced be to high regard,"
Said they, "and have our lady's love for his reward.

28

"Therefore announce sir, if thou have a love."
"Love have I sure," quoth she, "but lady none;
Yet will I not from mine own love remove,
Nor to your lady will I service do,
But wreak your wrongs wrought to this knight alone,
And prove his cause." With that her mortal spear
She mightily adventured towards one,
And down him smote, ere° well aware he aware,   *before*
Then to the next she rode, and down the next did bear.

29

Nor did she stay, till three on ground she laid,
That none of them himself could rise again;
The fourth was by that other knight dismayed,
All were he weary of his former pain,
That now there do but two of six remain;
Which two did yield, before she did them smite.
"Ah," said she then, "now may ye all see plain,
That truth is strong, and true love most of might,
That for his trusty servants doth so strongly fight."

30

"Too well we see," said they, "and prove too well
Our faulty weakness, and your matchless might:
Therefore, fair sir, yours be the damsel,
Which by her own law to your lot is won,
And we your liege men faith unto you pledge."
So underneath her feet their swords they marred,°   *dishonored*
And after her besought, well as they might,
To enter in, and reap the due reward:
She granted, and then in they all together fared.

31

Long were it to describe the goodly frame,
And stately port of Castle Joyeous,[23]
(For so that castle hight° by common name)   *was known*
Where they were entertained with courteous
And comely glee of many gracious
Fair ladies, and of many a gentle knight,
Who through a chamber long and spacious,
Quite soon them brought unto their lady's sight,
That of them claimed was the lady of delight.

32

But for to tell the sumptuous array
Of that great chamber, should be labor lost:

---

23. Come on, Castle Joyeous? That's like calling some park the "happiest place on earth." There will be tears.

For living wit, I ween,[24] cannot display
The royal riches and exceeding cost,
Of every pillar and of every post;
Which all of purest bullion framed were,
And with great pearls and precious stones embossed,
That the bright glister of their beams clear
Did sparkle forth great light, and glorious did appear.

33

These stranger knights through passing, forth were led
Into an inner room, whose royalty
And rich purveyance° might uneasily be told; *furniture*
Might Princes' palace so seem so decked to be.
Which stately manner when as they did see,
The image of superfluous riotous.[25]
Exceeding much the state of mean degree,
They greatly wondered, whence so sumptuous guise
Might be maintained, and each began diversely to guess.

34

The walls were round about appareled
With costly clothes of Arras and of Toure,° *exotic French tapestries*
In which with cunning hand was portrayed
The love of Venus and her paramour
The fair Adonis, turned to a flower,
A work of rare device, and wondrous wit.
First did it show the bitter baleful stowre,° *sorrowful trial*
Which her assailed with many a fervent fit,
When first her tender heart was with his beauty smitten.[26]

35

Then with what sleights and sweet allurements she
Enticed the boy, as well that art she knew,

---

24. To know. Remember it, because I can't keep doing this all day.
25. Here's a clue. Is a "superfluous" banquet a good thing?
26. The goddess Venus kidnapped and forced the boy Adonis to be her lover. Adonis was later killed by a boar and Venus turned him into a flower. This is the myth found on the tapestries. At the same time, though, we're actually learning the story of the queen of the castle, Malecasta and her "true" love.

And wooed him her paramour to be;
Now making garlands of each flower that grew,
To crown his golden locks with honor due;
Now leading him into a secret shade
From his Beauperes,[27] and from bright heaven's view,
Where him to sleep she gently would persuade,
Or bathe him in a fountain by some covert glade.

36

And whilst he slept, she over him would spread
Her mantle, colored like the starry skies,
And her soft arm lay underneath his head,
And with ambrosial kisses bathe his eyes;
And while he bathed, with her two crafty spies,
She secretly would search each dainty limb,
And throw into the well sweet rosemaries,
And fragrant violets, and pansies trim,
And ever with sweet Nectar she did sprinkle him.

37

So did she steal his heedless heart away,
And joyed his love in secret all unseen.
But for she saw him bent to cruel play,[28]
To hunt the savage beast in forest wide,
Dreadful° of danger, that might him betide,   *afraid*
She oft and oft advised him to refrain
From chase of greater beasts, whose brutish pride
Might cause him wounds unawares: but all in vain;
For who can shun the chance, that destiny doth ordain?

38

Lo, where beyond he lay languishing,
Deadly gored by a great wild Boar,
And by his side the goddess[29] groveling
Makes for him endless moan, and evermore
With her soft garment wipes away the gore,

---

27. Those he loved like brothers.
28. Like most knights of the time, he joyed in hunting the wild boar, as well.
29. This is Malecasta, whose name comes from the Latin words for "bad" and "chastity."

Which stains his snowy skin with hateful hue:
But when she saw no help might him restore,
Him to a dainty flower she did transmute,
Which in that cloth was wrought, as if it lively grew.

39

So was that chamber clad in goodly fashion,
And round about it many beds were ranged,
As in past was the antique world's passion,
Some for untimely ease, some for delight,
As pleased them to use, that use it might:
And all was full of damsels, and of squires,
Dancing and reveling both day and night,
And swimming deep in sensual desires,
And Cupid still amongst them kindled lustful fires.

40

And all the while sweet music did divide
Her looser notes with Lydian° harmony;   *wanton music of ancient origin*
And all the while sweet birds thereto applied
Their dainty lays and dulcet melody,
Ay caroling of love and jollity,
That wonder was to hear their trim consort.°   *pleasing harmony*
Which when those knights beheld, with scornful eye,
They disdained such lascivious disport,
And loathed the loose demeanor of that wanton sort.

41

Thence they were brought to that great lady's view,
Whom they found sitting on a sumptuous bed,
That glistered all with gold and glorious show,
As the proud Persian queen's accustomed:
She seemed a woman of great bounty,
And of rare beauty, saving that askance°   *suspiciously*
Her wanton eyes, ill signs of womanhood,[30]
Did roll too highly, and too often glance,
Without regard of grace, or comely amenability.

---

30. A woman's eyes should not roam as Malecasta's did.

42

Long work it were, and needless to describe
Their goodly entertainment and great glee:
She caused them be led in courteous ways
Into a bower,° disarmed for to be,   *a woman's private chamber*
And cheered well with wine and spices free:
The Redcross knight was soon disarmed there,[31]
But the brave maid[32] would not disarmed be,
But only vented up her visor there,
And so did let her goodly visage to appear.

43

As when fair Cynthia,[33] in darksome night,
Is in a noxious cloud enveloped,
Where she may find the substance thin and light,
Breaks forth her silver beams, and her bright head
Discovers of the world discomforted;
Of the poor traveler, who went astray,
With thousand blessings she is highly praised;
Such was the beauty and the shining ray,
With which fair Britomart gave light unto the day.

44

And also those six, which lately with her fought,
Now were disarmed, and did themselves present
Unto her view, and company unsought;
For they all seemed courteous and gentle,
And all six brethren, born of one parent,
Which had them trained in all civility,
And goodly taught to tilt° and tournament;   *joust*
Now were they liegemen° to this lady bright,   *servants*
And her knight's service ought,° to hold of her in right.   *owed*

---

31. The knight Britomart has just saved is Redcross (and so he was refusing to forswear Una). However, he seems to have fallen rather easily here. Um . . .
32. Britomart, our hero!
33. Cynthia is also known as Artemis, the virgin goddess of the moon and of the hunt. She was very beautiful. This is one of Spenser's techniques for saying something in a roundabout way; he's saying Britomart was lovely.

45

The first of them by name Gardante[34] hight,
A jolly person, and of comely view;
The second was Parlante,[35] a bold knight,
And next to him Jocante[36] did ensue;
Basciante[37] did himself most courteous show;
But fierce Bacchante[38] seemed too fierce and keen;
And yet in arms Noctante[39] greater grew:
All were fair knights, and goodly well beseen,
But to fair Britomart they all but shadows been.

46

For she was full of amiable grace,
And manly terror mixed there withal,
That as the one stirred up affections base,
So the other did men's rash desires appall,[40]
And hold them back, that would in error fall;
As he, that hath seen a vermillion rose,
To which sharp thorns and briars the way forestall,
Dare not for dread his hardy hand expose,
But wishing it far off, his idle wish doth lose.

47

Whom when the lady saw so fair a wight,°   *creature, meaning Britomart*
All ignorant of her contrary sex,
(For she her thought a fresh and lusty knight)
She greatly began enamored to wax,
And with vain thoughts her falsed fancy vex:
Her fickle heart conceived hasty fire,
Like sparks of fire, which fall in slender flax,°   *a flammable plant*
That shortly burned into extreme desire,
And ransacked all her veins with passion entire.

34. Now we're getting allegorical. Gardante means "Gazer." Tells you something about him.
35. Parlante means "Talker." Hmmm.
36. Jocante, as you can guess, means "Jokester" or "Playful."
37. Now we're getting serious. Basciate means "Kisser."
38. Bacchante means "Drinker."
39. "Night-lurker" might be a good substitute for the name for Noctante.
40. Britomart both attracts and scares the six knights.

48

And soon she grew to great impatience
And into terms of open outrage burst,
That plain discovered her incontinence,°   *impatience*
Nor reckoned she, who her meaning did mistrust;
For she was given all to fleshly lust,
And poured forth in sensual delight,
That all regard of shame she had discussed,
And meet respect of honor put to flight:
So shameless beauty soon becomes a loathsome sight.

49

Fair ladies, that to love captives are,
And chaste desires do nourish in your mind,
Let not her fault your sweet affections mar,
Nor blot the bounty of all womankind;
Amongst thousands good one wanton dame to find:
Amongst the roses grow some wicked weeds;
For this was not to love, but lust inclined;
For love does always bring forth bounteous deeds,
And in each gentle heart desire of honor breeds.

50

Not so of love this looser dame did skill,
But as a coal to kindle fleshly flame,
Giving the bridle to her wanton will,[41]
And treading under foot her honest name:
Such love is hate, and such desire is shame.
Still did she rove at her with crafty glance
Of her false eyes, that at her heart did aim,
And told her meaning in her countenance;
But Britomart dismissed it with ignorance.

51

Supper was shortly done and down they sat,
Where they were served with all sumptuous fare,
Whiles fruitful Ceres, and Lyæus[42] fat

---

41. She let her lusts range free.
42. Ceres was the goddess of agriculture; Lyæus (Bacchus) the god of the vine.

Poured out their plenty, without spite or sparing:
Naught was wanted there, that dainty was and rare;
And aye the cups their tables did overflow,
And aye between the cups, she did prepare
Way to her love, and secret darts did throw;
But Britomart would not such guileful message know.

52

So when they slaked had the fervent heat
Of appetite with meats of every sort,
The lady did fair Britomart entreat,
Her to disarm, and with delightful sport
To loose her warlike limbs and strong effort,
But when she might not thereunto be won,
(For she her sex under that strange disguise
Did use to hide, and plain appearance shun)
In plainer way to tell her grievance she began.

53

And all at once discovered her desire
With sighs, and sobs, and plaints, and piteous grief,
The outward sparks of her in burning fire;
Which spent in vain, at last she told her brief,
That but if she did lend her short relief,
And do her comfort, she might altogether die.
But the chaste damsel, that had never priefe°   *experience*
Of such malignant and subtle forgery,
Did easily believe her strong extremity.

54

Full easy was for her to have belief,
Who by self-feeling of her feeble sex,
And by long trial of the inward grief,
Wherewith imperious love her heart did vex,
Could judge what pains do loving hearts perplex.
Who means no guile, beguiled soonest shall,
And to fair semblance doth light faith annex;
The bird that knows not the false fowler's call,
Into his hidden net full easily doth fall.

55

Therefore, she would not in discourteous ways,
Scorn the fair offer of good will professed;
For great rebuke it is, love to despise,
Or rudely disdain a gentle heart's request;
But with fair countenance, as beseemed best,
Her entertained; nevertheless she inwardly deemed
Her love too light, to woo a wandering guest:
Which she misconstruing, thereby esteemed
That from like inward fire that outward smoke had steamed.[43]

56

Therewith awhile she[44] her fleet fancy fed,
Till she might win the right time for her desire,
But yet her wound still inward freshly bled,[45]
And through her bones the false instilled fire
Did spread itself, and venom close inspire.°   *stimulate, create*
Though were the tables taken all away,
And every knight, and every gentle Squire
Began choose his dame with basciomani° gay,   *a kiss on the hand*
With whom he meant to make his sport and courtly play.

57

Some fell to dance, some fell to hazardry,°   *gambling*
Some to make love, some to make merriment,
As diverse wits to divers things apply;
And all the while fair Malecasta bent
Her crafty engines° to her close intent.   *plans*
By this the eternal lamps, wherewith high Jove[46]
Doth light the lower world, were half spent,
And the moist daughters of huge Atlas strove
Into the Ocean deep to drive their weary drove.[47]

---

43. At this point, Britomart's a bit naive and doesn't realize how insincere and lustful Malecasta is, especially since she is enduring so much for her own true love.
44. Remember, we're talking about Malecasta here.
45. Spenser speaks of Malecasta's lust as a sickness, an inward cancer.
46. It's bedtime.
47. The daughters of Atlas, the Hyades, were a constellation of seven stars who drove their chariots across the sky.

58

High time it seemed then for every wight
Them to betake unto their kindly rest;
And soon long waxen torches were light,
Unto their bowers to guide every guest:
Though when the Britoness° saw all the rest   *Britomart*
Withdrawing quite, she began to steal away
And safe commit to her soft feathered nest,
Where through long watch, and late days weary toil,
She soundly slept, and careful thoughts did quite absolve.

59

Now when all the world in silence deep
Shrouded was, and every mortal wight
Was drowned in the depth of deadly sleep,
Fair Malecasta, whose engrieved spirit
Could find no rest in such perplexed plight,
Lightly arose out of her weary bed,
And under the black veil of guilty night,
Her with a scarlet mantle covered,
That was with gold and ermines° fair enveloped.   *black furs*

60

Then panting soft, and trembling every joint,
Her fearful feet towards the bower she moved;
Where she for secret purpose did appoint
To lodge the warlike maid unwisely loved,[48]
And to her bed approaching, first she proved,°   *tested*
Whether she slept or waked, with her soft hand
She softly felt, if any member moved,
And lent her wary ear to understand,
If any puff of breath, or sign of sense she found.

61

Which when none she found, with easy shift,
For fear lest her unawares she should cause fear,
The embroidered quilt she lightly up did lift,

---

48. Remember, she still doesn't realize Britomart is a woman.

And by her side herself she softly laid,
Of every finest fingers touch afraid;
Nor any noise she made, nor word she spoke,
But inwardly sighed. At last the royal maid
Out of her quiet slumber did awake,
And changed her weary side, the better ease to take.

62

Where feeling one close couched by her side,
She lightly leapt out of her filed bed,
And to her weapon ran, in mind to strike
The loathed lecher. But the Dame half-dead
Through sudden fear and ghastly dread,
Did shriek aloud, that through the house it rang,
And the whole family therewith dread,
Rashly out of their roused couches sprang,
And to the troubled chamber all in arms did throng.

63

And those six knights (that lady's champions),
And also Redcross knight ran to the sound,
Half armed and half unarmed, with them at once:
Where when confusedly they came, they found
Their lady lying on the senseless ground;
On the other side, they saw the warlike maid
All in her snow-white smock, with locks unbound,
Threatening the point of her avenging blade,
That with so troubling terror they were all dismayed.

64

About their lady first they flocked around,
Whom having laid in comfortable couch,
Shortly they reared out of her frozen swoon;
And afterward began with foul reproach
To stir up strife, and troublous contentions words:
But by example of the last day's loss,
None of them rashly dared to approach,
Nor in so glorious spoil themselves embellish;
She aided likewise by the champion of the bloody cross.

65

But one of those six knights, Gardante hight,
Drew out a deadly bow and arrow keen,
Which forth he sent with felonous° despite,   *wicked*
And fell intent against the virgin sheen:°   *shining*
The mortal steel stayed not, till it was seen
To gore her side, yet was the wound not deep,
But lightly grazed her soft silken skin,
That drops of purple blood thereout did weep,
Which did her lily smock with stains of vermilion seep.

66

Wherewith enraged she fiercely at them flew,
And with her flaming sword about her laid,
That none of them foul mischief could eschew,°   *avoid*
But with her dreadful strokes were all dismayed:
Here, there, and everywhere about her swayed
Her wrathful steel, that none might it abide;
And so the Redcross knight gave her good aid,
And joining foot to foot, and side to side,
That in short space their foes they have quite terrified.

67

Though when all were put to shameful flight,
The noble Britomartis her arrayed,
And her bright arms about her body dight:°   *readied to leave*
For nothing would she longer there be stayed,
Where so loose life, and so ungentle trade
Was used of knights and ladies seeming gent:
So early, ere the gross earth's gray morn
Was all dispersed out of the firmament,
They took their steeds, and forth upon their journey went.

WORD PLAY

Match the Spenserian words to their modern meanings.

trains	*piercing*
allured	*trial*
assay	*plans*
yode	*dwell*
wone	*creature*
pricked	*persuaded*
poignant	*seriously*
rived	*splintered*
sore	*rode forth*
wight	*spurred*

DISCUSSION QUESTIONS

1. Spenser begins by writing of Queen Elizabeth I's "perfection." Why do you think this is?

2. Malecasta had a true love once, but he died. How has she behaved since? What is Spenser telling us about chastity here?

3. Initially, what traits do you find in Britomart? If she is to be our model of chastity, what does this say about chastity?

Canto II.

*The Redcrosse knight to Britomart
describes Artegal;
The wondrous mirage,° by which she   image, reflection
in love with him did fall.[1]*

1

Here have I[2] cause, in men just blame to find,
That in their proper praise too partial be,
And not indifferent° to woman kind,   *just, fair*
To whom no share in arms and chivalry
They do impart, nor make memory
Of their brave gestures and prowess martial;
Scarce do they spare to one or two or three,
Room in their writs;° yet the same writing small   *writings*
Does all their deeds deface,[3] and dims their glories all.

2

But by record of antique times I find,
That women wont° in wars to bear most sway,[4]   *accustomed*
And to all great exploits themselves inclined:
Of which they still the garland bore away,
Till envious men fearing their rule's decay,
Began enact strict laws to curb their liberty;
Yet since they warlike arms have laid away:

---

1. Just a note here: in Cantos II and III, we're going to learn about Britomart's past—how she became a knight (and why), and how she obtained her armor and magic spear. It's something of a Spenserian flashback.
2. This is Spenser speaking, lamenting that men don't praise women adequately, especially when it comes to war.
3. And to Glorianna, men give too little praise.
4. Here, he could be speaking of the Amazons, a race of warrior women.

They have excelled in arts and policy,
That now we foolish men that praise begin also to envy.

3

Of warlike puissance in ages spent,
Be thou fair Britomart, whose praise I write,
But of all wisdom be thou precedent,°   *first, foremost*
O sovereign Queen, whose praise I would write,
And write I would as duty doth excite;
But ah, my rhymes too rude and rugged are,
When in so high an object they do alight,
And striving, fit to make, I fear do mar:
Thyself thy praises tell, and make them known quite far.

4

She traveling with Guyon by the way,
Of sundry things fair purpose began to find,
To abridge° their journey long, and lingering day;   *shorten*
Amongst which it fell into that Faery's[5] mind,
To ask this Briton maid, what uncouth wind,
Brought her into those parts, and what quest
Made her dissemble° her disguised kind: *hide*
Fair lady she him seemed, like lady dressed,
But fairest knight alive, when armed was her breast.

5

Thereat she sighing softly, had no power
To speak a while, nor ready answer make,
But with heart-thrilling° throbs and bitter stowre,°   *piercing / sorrow*
As if she had a fever fit, did quake,
And every dainty limb with horror shake;[6]
And ever and soon the rosy red,
Flashed through her face, as it had been a flash
Of lightning, through bright heaven in protest;
At last the passion passed, she thus him answered:

---

5. Redcrosse knight is now going to question her.
6. Come on, she's tough. I can't picture her trembling in every dainty limb.

6

"Fair Sir, I let you weet, that from the hour
I taken was from nurse's tender pap,⁷
I have been trained up in warlike pains,
To use the spear and shield, and to strike down
The warlike rider to his most mishap;
Since then I loathed have my life to lead,
As ladies wont,° in pleasure's wanton lap,   *are used to*
To finger the fine needle and nice thread;
I'd liefer° were with point of foe-man's spear be dead.⁸   *rather*

7

"All my delight on deeds of arms is set,
To hunt out perils and adventures hard,
By sea, by land, where so they may be met,
Only for honor and for high regard,
Without respect of riches or reward.
For such intent into these parts I came,
Without a compass, or without a card,
Far from my native soil, that is by name
The greater Britain, here to seek for praise and fame.

8

"Fame blazed hath, that here in Faery land
Do many famous knights and ladies won,
And many strange adventures to be found,
Of which great worth and worship may be won,
Which I to prove, this voyage have begun.
But might I weet of you, right courteous knight,⁹
Tidings of one, that hath unto me done
Late foul dishonor and reproachful spite,
The which I seek to wreak, and Artegall¹⁰ he hight."¹¹

---

7. In this case, it means her nurse's care.
8. Personally, I feel the same way about needlepoint.
9. Aha! Now we're getting to the point of her story. She wants to know about a certain someone.
10. Now, Spenser being Spenser, he spells this name as "Arthegall," "Artegal," "Artegall," and "Arthegal," at different times. Yes, differently within the same Canto even. We will use Artegall because that's how it is spelled in Book V.
11. She's not really mad at him. She seeks to know more about his character and his honor.

9

The word gone out, she back again would call,
As her repenting so to have misspoke,
But that he it up-taking ere the fall,
Her shortly answered; "Fair martial maid
Certainly, ye misinformed have been, to upbraid
A gentle knight with so unknightly blame:
For weet ye well of all, that ever played
At tilt or tourney,° or like warlike game,   *joust*
The noble Artegall hath ever borne the name.

10

"For thy great wonder were it, if such shame
Should ever enter in his bounteous thought,
Or ever do, that might deserve some blame:
The noble courage never knoweth ought,
That may unworthy of itself be thought.
Therefore, fair damsel, be ye well aware,
Lest that too far ye have your sorrow sought:
You and your country both I wish welfare,
And honor both; for each of other worthy are."

11

The royal maid grew inwardly wondrous glad,
To hear her love so highly magnified,
And joyed that ever she affixed had,
Her heart on knight so goodly glorified,
However finely she it feigned to hide:
The loving mother, that nine months did bear,
In the dear closet of her painful side,
Her tender babe, it seeing safe appear,
Doth not so much rejoice, as she[12] rejoiced there.

12

But to occasion him to further talk,
To feed her humor with his pleasing style,

---

12. Britomart was as overjoyed as Artegall's own mother would've been at his birth.

Her list° in quarrelsome terms with him to balk,°¹³   *wish / hesitate*
And thus replied: "However, sir, ye file°   *arrange*
Your courteous tongue, his praises to compile,
It ill becomes a knight of gentle sort,
Such as ye have him boasted, to beguile
A simple maid, and work so heinous tort,°   *injury*
In shame of knighthood, as I largely can report.

13

"Let be therefore my vengeance to dissuade,
And learn, where I that impostor false may find."
"Ah, but if reason fair might you persuade,
To slake your wrath, and mollify your mind,"
Said he, "Perhaps ye should it better find:
For hardy thing it is, to ween by might,
That man to hard conditions to bind,
Or ever hope to match in equal fight,
Whose prowess paragon saw never living wight.

14

"Nor truly is it easy for to learn,
Where now on earth, or how he may be found;
For he nor won in one certain stead,¹⁴
But restless walk all the world around,
And doing things, that to his fame renown,
Defending ladies' cause, and orphans' right,
Where so he hears, that any doth confound
Them comfortless, through tyranny or might:
So is his sovereign honor raised to heaven's hight."¹⁵

15

His feeling words her feeble sense much pleased,
And softly sunk into her molten heart;
Heart that is inwardly hurt, is greatly eased
With hope of thing, that may allege° his smart;   *assuage*

---

13. In other words, she intended to speak to him in such a way as to make him more careful with his words.
14. He won neither a castle nor a place in a court.
15. Remember, "name."

For pleasing words are like to magic art,
That doth the charmed snake in slumber lay:
Such secret ease felt gentle Britomart,
Yet listed the same force with feigned wrong;
So discord oft in music makes the sweeter song.

16

And said: "Sir knight, these idle terms forbear,
And since it is uneasy to find his haunt,°   *abode*
Tell me some marks,[16] by which he may appear,
If chance I him encounter paramount;°   *peradventure*
For indeed one shall other slay, or daunt:
What shape, what shield, what arms, what steed, what steadfastness,
And what so else his person most may vaunt?"
All which the Redcross knight to point relayed,
And him in every part before her fashioned.

17

Yet him in every part before she knew,
How ever list° her now her knowledge fain°,   *wish / desirous*
Since him in past in Britain she did view,
To her revealed in a mirror plain,[17]
Whereof did grow her first added pain;
Whose root and stalk so bitter yet did taste,
That but the fruit more sweetness did contain,
Her wretched days in dolor° she might waste,   *sorrow*
And yield the prey of love to loathsome death at last.[18]

18

By strange occasion she did him behold,
And much more strangely began to love his sight,
As it in books hath written been of old.
In Deheubarth that now South Wales is hight,°   *a kingdom now part of Wales*
What time King Ryence° reigned, and dealt right,   *a legendary Welsh king*
The great magician Merlin had devised,

16. Physical traits.
17. A special mirror: we'll learn more about it.
18. Seeing Artegall has led to a lot of painful but pleasant feelings at first (a bitter stalk), and she will die in sorrow unless she finds him and a correspondingly greater joy (a sweet fruit).

By his deep science, and hell-dreaded might,
A looking glass, right wondrously glazed,
Whose virtues through the wide world soon were solemnized.

19

It virtue had, to show in perfect sight,
What ever thing was in the world contained,
Betwixt the lowest earth and heaven's height,
So that it to the looker appertained;
Whatever foe had wrought, or friend had feigned,
Therein discovered was, nor ought might pass,
Nor ought in secret from the same remained;
For that it round and hollow shaped was,
Like to the world itself,[19] and seemed a world of glass.

20

Who wonders not, that knows so wondrous work?
But who does wonder, that has known the tower,
Wherein the Egyptian Phao[20] long did lurk
From all men's view, that none might her discover,
Yet she might all men view out of her bower?
Great Ptolomæ[21] it for his lover's sake
Built all of glass, by magic power,
And also it impregnable did make;
Yet when his love was false, he with a piece it broke.

21

Such was the glassy globe that Merlin made,
And gave unto King Ryence for his guard,
That never foes his kingdom might invade,
But he it knew at home before he heard
Tidings thereof, and so them still debarred.
It was a famous present for a prince,
And worthy work of infinite reward,
That treasons couldn't betray, and foes convince;
Happy this realm, had it remained ever since.

---

19. Spenser obviously hadn't learned the earth is flat. Trust me on this.
20. One of Ptolemy's lovers.
21. You know, the Greco-Roman astronomer.

22

One day it fortuned, fair Britomart
Into her father's closet to retire;
For nothing he from her reserved apart,
Being his only daughter and his heir;
Where when she had espied that mirror fair,
Herself a while therein she viewed in vanity;
Though her assessment of the virtues rare,
Which thereof spoken were, she began again
Her to bethink of, that might to herself pertain.[22]

23

But as it falleth, in the gentlest hearts
Imperious love hath highest set his throne,
And tyrannize in the bitter pains
Of them, that to him buxom° are and prone:[23]   *acquiescent*
So thought this maid (as maidens used to done)
Whom fortune for her husband would allot,
Not that she lusted after any one;
For she was pure from blame of sinful blot,
Yet knew her life at last must link in that same knot.

24

And soon there was presented to her eye
A comely knight, all armed in complete ways,[24]
Through whose bright visor lifted up on high
His manly face, that did his foes dread,
And friends to terms of gentle truce entice,
Looked forth, as Phoebus' face out of the east,°   *the sunrise (in this case)*
Betwixt two shady mountains doth arise;
Portly° his person was, and much increased   *not fat, but burly*
Through his heroic grace, and honorable jousts.

25

His crest was covered with a couchant hound,[25]
And all his armor seemed of antique mold,

---

22. She worried about modesty.
23. Love is not prideful.
24. This is Artegall.
25. His shield displayed a hound resting on its hind legs. Its head is raised, signifying attentiveness.

Edmund Spenser, the Prince of Poets

Edmund Spenser was born in either 1552 or 1553 in London. He received a classical education at the Merchant Taylors School. Spenser attended college at Pembroke Hall, Cambridge University, receiving a bachelor of arts degree in 1573 and a master of arts degree in 1576.

He first went to work for the Bishop of Rochester (John Young). He then served under the Earl of Leicester, Robert Dudley. In 1580 he was appointed secretary to the Lord Deputy of Ireland. In 1581, Ireland became his home. He eventually acquired an estate called Kilcolman (complete with a castle), near the cities of Cork and Limerick.

Spenser was married twice. He married Machabyas Chylde in 1579. In 1594 she died, and he married Elizabeth Boyle.

Spenser's first published works were verses he helped translate while still at the Merchant Taylors School. (They form a long allegorical poem, called *The Theatre for Worldlings,* by Jan van der Noodt.)

His first independent work was published in 1579. It was *The Shepheardes Calendar,* a "pastoral" poem quite fashionable in literary circles then.

The Faerie Queene was his greatest work, and he began it in 1580. But even his friends looked down on it. Until Spenser came along, English was not thought to be a suitable language for an epic poem. However, in the ten years he spent preparing the first three books, he never lost faith in his poem.

And after the first three books were published (in part) in 1591, he was rewarded by Queen Elizabeth (to whom the poem is dedicated) with a yearly stipend of fifty pounds.

The next three books were published in 1596, along with another poem, "Fowre Hymnes."

In 1598, rebels in Ireland rose up, led by the Earl of Tyrone, in an attempt to wrest control of Ireland from the English. Though the rebellion eventually failed, Spenser's estate, Kilcolman, was captured by the rebels. He was forced to seek shelter in Cork. From there, he carried a bundle of letters from the Lord Deputy to the Privy Council (the queen's advisors). He arrived in Westminster on Christmas Eve, 1598. He died there on January 13, 1599.

He is buried in Westminster Abbey, and inscribed on his tomb are the words, "The Prince of Poets."

But wondrous massive and assured soundness,
And round about adorned all with gold,
In which there written was with ciphers old,
Achilles' armor, which Artegall did win.[26]
And on his shield enveloped sevenfold
He bore a crowned ermine,[27]
That decked the azure[28] field with her fair treated skin.

26

The damsel well did view his personage,
And liked well, nor further fixed her gaze not,
But went her way; nor her guiltless age
Did ween, unawares, that her unlucky lot
Lay hidden in the bottom of the pot;[29]
Of hurt unknown most danger doth redound:°   *returning*
But the false archer,° which that arrow shot   *Cupid*
So slyly, that she did not feel the wound,
Did smile full smoothly at her unknowing woeful pain.

27

Thenceforth the feather in her lofty crest,
Ruffed of love, began lowly to avail,
And her proud importance, and her princely jousts,
With which she earnestly triumphed, now did quail[30]
Sad, solemn, sorrow, and full of fancies frail
She waxed; yet knew she neither how, nor why,
She knew not, silly maid, what she did ail,
Yet beknownst, she was not well at ease in folly,
Yet thought it was not love, but some melancholy.

28

So soon as night had with her pallid hew
Defaced the beauty of the shining sky,
And cleft from men the world's desired view,

---

26. Remember, Spenser was attempting to link his epic to history—or pseudo-history.
27. Like mink, it's a fur that signifies status.
28. The color blue, also signifying status.
29. Spenser could be referring to Pandora's Box, which contained much woe but hope at last.
30. She began to become distracted, to lose jousts, and to lose her focus. Sounds like high school to me.

She with her nurse down to sleep did lie;
But sleep full far away from her did fly:
Instead thereof sad sighs, and sorrows deep
Kept watch and ward about her warily,
That naught she did but wail, and often steep[31]
Her dainty couch with tears, which closely she did weep.

29

And if that any drop of slumbering rest
Did chance to still into her weary spirit,
When feeble nature felt herself oppressed,
Straight way with dreams, and with fantastic sight
Of dreadful things the same was put to flight,
That oft out of her bed she did start,
As one with view of ghastly fiends affright:
Began she to renew her former smart,°   *pain*
And think of that fair visage, written in her heart.

30

One night, when she was tossed with such unrest,
Her aged nurse, whose name was Glauce hight,[32]
Feeling her leap out of her loathed nest,
Betwixt her feeble arms her quickly caught,
And down again in her warm bed her brought;
"Ah my dear daughter, ah my dearest dread,
What uncouth fit," said she, "what evil plight
Hath thee oppressed, and with sad dreary dread
Changed thy lively cheer, and living made thee dead?

31

"For not of naught these sudden ghastly fear
All night afflict thy natural repose,
And all the day, when as thine equal peers,
Their fit disports° with fair delight do chose,   *pastimes*
Thou in dull corners does thyself enclose,[33]
Nor tastes princes' pleasures, nor does spread

---

31. She drenched her couch with tears.
32. Glauce was also the name of Zeus's nurse.
33. She cut herself off from the world.

Abroad thy fresh youth's fairest flower, but lose
Both leaf and fruit, both too untimely shed,
As one in willful bale° for ever buried.³⁴   *affliction*

32

"The time, that mortal men their weary cares
Do lay away, and all wild beasts do rest,
And every river eke his course forbears
Then doth this wicked evil thee infest,
And rive° with thousand throbs thy thrilled breast;   *burst*
Like an huge Aenta° of deep engulfed grief,   *Mount Etna*
Sorrow is heaped in thy hollow chest,
Whenceforth it breaks in sighs and anguish rife,°   *full*
As smoke and sulfur° mingled with confused strife.   *evil vapors*

33

"Aye me, how much I fear, lest love it be;
But if that love it be, as sure I read
By knowing signs and passions, which I see,
Be it worthy of thy race and royal seed,
Then I avow by this most sacred head
Of my dear foster child, to ease thy grief!
For death nor danger from thy due relief
Shall me bar, tell me therefore my liefest liefe."°   *my beloved one*

34

So having said, her between her arms two
She straightly strained, and cooled tenderly,
And every trembling joint, and every vein
She softly felt, and rubbed busily,
To do the frozen cold away to fly;
And her fair dewy eyes with kisses dear
She oft did bathe, and oft again did dry;
And ever her importuned,° not to fear   *urged*
To let the secret of her heart to her appear.

---

34. This is a common Renaissance theme. Beauty should not be hidden away; it should be made the object of chaste love.

35

The damsel paused, and then thus fearfully;
"Ah Nurse, what need thee to eke° my pain? *share*
Is not enough, that I alone do die,
But it must doubled be with death of two?
For naught for me but death there doth remain."
"O daughter dear," said she, "despair not a bit;
For never sore, but might a salve obtain:
That blinded god,° which hath ye blindly smote, *Cupid*
Another arrow hath your lover's heart to hit."

36

"But mine is not," quoth she,[35] "like other's wound;
For which no reason can find remedy."
"Was never such, but might the like be found,"
Said she,[36] "and though no reason may apply
Salve to your sore, yet love can higher soar,
Than reason's reach, and oft hath wonders done.
"But neither god of love, nor God of sky
Can do," said she, "that, which cannot be done."
"Things oft impossible," quoth she "seem, ere begun."

37

"These idle words," said she, "do naught assuage
My stubborn smart,° but more annoyance breed, *pain*
For no, no usual fire, no usual rage
It is, O nurse, which on my life doth feed,
And sucks the blood, which from my heart doth bleed.[37]
But since thy faithful zeal lets me not hide
My crime, (if crime it be) I will it plead.
Nor prince, nor peer it is, whose love hath ground
My feeble breast of late, and launched this wound wide.

38

"Nor man it is, nor other living wight;
For then some hope I might unto me draw,

---

35. Britomart is speaking now.
36. Back to the nurse . . .
37. Britomart's love isn't a usual kind of love, since she has never truly seen (in the flesh) the object of her affection.

But only shade and semblance of a knight,
Whose shape or person yet I never saw,
Hath me subjected to love's cruel law:
The same one day, as me misfortune led,
I in my father's wondrous mirror saw,
And pleased with that seeming goodly-hed,°   *graciousness*
Unawares the hidden hook with bait I swallowed.

39

"Since it hath in-fixed faster° hold   *firmer*
Within my bleeding bowels, and so sore
Now rankles° in this same frail fleshly mold,   *fester*
That all mine entrails flow with poisonous gore,[38]
And the ulcer grows daily more and more;
Nor can my running sore find remedy,
Other than my hard fortune to deplore,
And languish as the leaf fallen from the tree,
Till death make one end of my days and misery."

40

"Daughter," said she,[39] "what need ye be dismayed,
Or why make ye such monster of your mind?
Of much more uncouth thing I was afraid;
Of filthy lust, contrary unto kind:°   *nature*
But this affection nothing strange I find;
For who with reason can you aye reprove,
To love the semblance° pleasing most your mind,   *image*
And yield your heart, whence ye cannot remove?
No guilt in you, but in the tyranny of love.

41

"Not so the Arabian Myrrhe[40] did set her mind;
Nor so did Biblis spend her pining heart,
But loved their native flesh against all kind,

---

38. Her point is she is wasting away from within because of this impossible love.
39. Nurse again. Getting the hang of this?
40. Myrrhe, Biblis and Pasiphaë are examples Glauce, the nurse, uses to soothe Britomart about unusual love. Myrrhe loved her father; Biblis, her brother; and Pasiphaë, a cow. Britomart's love for a man whom she has never seen, though unusual, is natural.

And to their purpose used wicked art:
Yet played Pasiphaë a more monstrous part,
That loved a bull, and learned a beast to be;
Such shameful lusts who loathes not, which depart
From course of nature and of modesty?
Sweet love such lewdness bans from his fair company.

42

"But thine my dear (well fare thy heart my dear)
Though strange beginning had, yet fixed is
On one, that worthy may perhaps appear;
And certainly seems bestowed not amiss:[41]
Joy thereof have thou and eternal bliss."
With that up-leaning on her elbow weak,
Her alabaster breast she soft did kiss,
Which all that while she felt to pant and quake,
As it an earthquake were; at last she° thus bespoke.   *Britomart*

43

"Grandmother, your words do work me little ease;
For though my love be not so lewdly bent,
As those ye blame, yet may it naught appease
My raging smart, nor ought my flame relent,
But rather doth my helpless grief augment.
For they, however shameful and unkind,
Yet did possess their horrible intent:
Short end of sorrows they thereby did find;
So was their fortune good, though wicked were their mind.[42]

44

"But wicked fortune mine, though mind be good,
Can have no end, nor hope of my desire,
But feed on shadows, whiles I die for food,
And like a shadow wax,° whiles with entire   *to grow*
Affection, I do languish and expire.
I fonder than Narcissus, foolish child,
Who having viewed in a fountain sheer

---

41. Her lover may appear, and her love seems not to be misdirected.
42. The examples cited by the nurse (Glauce) all died quickly; Britomart sees this as a relief.

His face, was with the love thereof beguiled;
I fonder love a shade,° the body far exiled." *ghost, spirit*

45

"Naught like," quoth she, "for that same wretched boy
Was of himself the idle paramour;° *lover*
Both love and lover, without hope of joy,[43]
For which he faded to a watery flower.
But better fortune thine, and better hour,
Which loves the shadow of a warlike knight;
No shadow, but a body hath in power:
That body, wheresoever that it light,
May learned be by ciphers, or by magic might.

46

"But if thou may with reason yet repress
The growing evil, ere it strength have got,
And thee abandoned wholly do possess,
Against it strongly strive, and yield thee not,
Till thou in open field down be smote.
But if the passion master thy frail might,
So that needs love or death must be thy lot,
Then I avow to thee, by wrong or right
To accomplish thy desire, and find that loved knight."

47

Her cheerful words much cheered the feeble spirit
Of the sick virgin, that her down she laid
In her warm bed to sleep, if that she might;
And the old woman carefully displayed
The bedclothes about her round with busy aid;
So that at last a little creeping sleep
Surprised her sense: she therewith well darken,
The drunken[44] lamp down in the oil did steep,
And set her by to watch, and set her by to weep.

---

43. In Christian theology, the Trinity is the perfect example of love. There is the Lover (God the Father), the Beloved (God the Son), and the Love itself (the Holy Spirit). Narcissus symbolizes love of self—incomplete, unwholesome love.
44. It means "liquid."

48

Early the morrow next, before that day
His° joyous face did to the world reveal,   *the sun*
They both rose up and took their ready way
Unto the church, their prayers to appeal,
With great devotion, and with little zeal:
For the fair damsel from the holy rehearsal[45]
Her love-sick heart to other thoughts did steal;
And that old dame said many an idle verse,[46]
Out of her daughter's heart fond fancies to reverse.

49

Returned home, the royal infant fell[47]
Into her former fit; for why, no power
Nor guidance of herself in her did dwell.
But the aged nurse her calling to her bower,
Had gathered rew, and savine, and the flower
Of camphara, and calamint, and dill,[48]
All which she in a earthen pot did pour,
And to the brim with colt wood did it fill,
And many drops of milk and blood through it did spill.

50

Then taking thrice three[49] hairs from off her head,
Them triply braided in a threefold lace,
And round about the pot's mouth, bound the thread,
And after having whispered a space
Certain sad words, with hollow voice and bass,
She to the virgin said, thrice said she it;
"Come daughter come, come; spit upon my face,[50]
Spit thrice upon me, thrice upon me spit;
The uneven number for this business is most fit."

---

45. Probably, her confession to God.
46. Protestants didn't have much respect for the repetitive prayers of the Catholics; that could be what he means by "idle verse."
47. I *dare* you to call Britomart an "infant."
48. The ingredients aren't important here. The issue is the brewing of a potion. Spenser saw this as an attempt by mortals to do God's job in healing a wounded heart.
49. By my college math, that's nine. Just saying.
50. Ew.

51

That said, her round about she from her turned,
She turned her contrary to the sun,
Thrice she her turned contrary, and returned,
All contrary, for she the right did shun,
And ever what she did, was straight undone.
So thought she to undo her daughter's love:[51]
But love, that is in gentle breast begun,
No idle charms so lightly may remove,
That well can witness, who by trial it does prove.

52

Nor ought it might the noble maid avail,
Nor slake the fury of her cruel flame,
But that she still did waste, and still did wail,
That through long languor, and heart-burning brame°   *passion*
She shortly like a pined ghost became,
Which long hath waited by the Stygian strand.[52]
That when old Glauce saw, for fear lest blame
Of her miscarriage should in her be found,
She knew not how to amend, nor how it to withstand.

---

51. For Artegall.
52. The shore of the River Styx.

WORD PLAY

Match the Spenserian words to their modern meanings.

wont	*hesitate*
stowre	*accustomed*
thrilling	*named*
balk	*sorrow*
file	*abode*
tort	*piercing*
hight	*blue*
haunt	*injury*
dolor	*arrange*
azure	*sorrow*

DISCUSSION QUESTIONS

1. Britomart pretends to be an enemy of Artegall's. Why do you suppose she does so?

2. Why does Britomart deny to her nurse that she is in love with Artegall?

3. Why didn't the nurse's potions work on Britomart?

ANTO III.

Merlin bewrays° to Britomart,   *shows*
the state of Artegal.
And shows the famous progeny°   *race, people*
which from them springen shall.

1

Most sacred fire, that burnest mightily
In living breasts, kindled first above,
Amongst the eternal spheres and lighting sky,
And thence poured into men, which men call love;
Not that same, which doth base affections move
In brutish minds, and filthy lust inflame,
But that sweet fit, that doth true beauty love,
And chose virtue for his dearest dame,
Whence spring all noble deeds and never dying fame:

2

Well did antiquity a god thee deem,[1]
That over mortal minds has so great might,
To order them, as best to thee doth seem,
And all their actions to direct aright;
The fatal° purpose of divine foresight,   *set by fate*
Thou does effect in destined descents,[2]
Through deep impression of thy secret might,
And stirred up the heroes' high intents,[3]
Which the late world admires for wondrous monuments.°   *achievements*

---

1. The ancients (Greeks, Romans, etc.) considered Love a god, hence Cupid and Aphrodite.
2. Direct descendants. You know, children and grandchildren.
3. Love makes even brave men do stupid things.

3

But thy[4] dread darts in none do triumph more,
Nor braver proof in any, of thy power
Shrewdest thou, than in this royal maid of yore,
Making her seek an unknown paramour,°   *lover*
From the world's end, through many a bitter sorrow:
From whose two loins thou afterward did raise
Most famous fruits of matrimonial bower,[5]
Which through the earth have spread their living praise,
That fame in trumpets of gold eternally displays.

4

Begin then, O my dearest sacred dame,
Daughter of Phoebus and of Memory,[6]
That does ennoble with immortal name
The warlike Worthies, from antiquity,[7]
In thy great volume of eternity:
Begin, O Clio, and recount from hence
My glorious Sovereign's goodly ancestry,
Till that by due degrees and long pretense,
Thou have it lastly brought unto her Excellence.[8]

5

Full many ways within her troubled mind,
Old Glauce cast, to cure this lady's grief:
Full many ways she sought, but none could find,
Nor herbs, nor charms, nor counsel, that is chief
And choicest medicine for sick heart's relief:
For thy great care she took, and greater fear,
Lest that it should her turn to foul reproof,

---

4. Love's.
5. I.e., the English nation.
6. Spenser means his poetic muse.
7. Classical reference: The "Worthies" were nine righteous men; their names varied according to the list.
8. Okay, here's what's going to happen. Just as Virgil did in the *Aeneid* with Caesar, Spenser is attempting to trace Elizabeth I's bloodline back to Britomart. It will be long, and it will be a little complicated. In many versions, including the Everyman edition, they skip this whole Canto with a summary. I'm going to include it and leave the decision to you.

CANTO III.

And sore reproach, when so her father dear
Should of his dearest daughter's hard misfortune hear.

6

At last she her advised, that he,[9] which made
That mirror, wherein the sick damsel
So strangely viewed her strange lover's shade,
To wit, the learned Merlin, well could tell,
Under what coast of heaven the man did dwell,
And by what means his love might best be wrought:
For though beyond the African Ishmael,[10]
Or the Indian Peru[11] he were, she thought
Him forth through infinite endeavor to have sought.

7

Forthwith themselves, disguising both in strange
And base attire, that none might them betray,
To Maridunum, that is now by changed
In name Cayr-Merdin[12] called, they tooke their way:
There the wise Merlin formerly was used (they say)
To make his home, low underneath the ground,
In a deep delve, far from the view of day,
That of no living wight he might be found,
When so he counseled with his spirits encompassed round.

8

And if thou ever happen that same way
To travel, go to see that dreadful place:
It is an hideous hollow cave (they say)
Under a rock that lays a little space
From the swift Barry,[13] tumbling down apace,
Amongst the woody hills of Dynevor:
But dare thou not, I charge, in any case,

---

9. Merlin, remember?
10. The northern part of Africa was thought to have been colonized by Ishmael.
11. The New World was already discovered, and Elizabeth's sailors were exploring its bounds (and wealth).
12. Carmarthen in Wales (actually, Arthur began as a Welsh legend).
13. The old name of a Welsh river.

To enter into that same baleful bower,
For fear the cruel fiends should thee unawares devour.

9

But standing high aloft, low lay thine ear,
And there such ghastly noise of iron chains,
And brass cauldrons thou shalt rumbling hear,
Which thousand spirits with long enduring pains
Do toss, that it will stun thy feeble brains,
And oftentimes great groans, and grievous shocks,
When too huge toil and labor them constrains:
And oftentimes loud strokes, and ringing sounds
From under that deep rock most horribly rebounds.

10

The cause some say is this: A little while
Before that Merlin died, he did intend,
A brass wall encompassing to compile
About Cairmardin,° and did it commend   *his cavern*
Unto these spirits, to bring to perfect end.
During which work the Lady of the Lake,[14]
Whom long he loved, for him in haste did send,
Who thereby forced his workmen to forsake,
Them bound till his return, their labor not to slake.

11

In the meantime through that false lady's tricks,
He was surprised, and buried under bier[15]
Nor ever to his work returned again:[16]
Nevertheless those fiends may not their work forbear,
So greatly his commandment they fear,
But there do toil and travail day and night,

---

14. According to legend, the Lady of the Lake enchanted Merlin by entrapping him in a tree after he had taught her all his magical knowledge. Dames. Other legends say she gave Arthur his sword, Excalibur.
15. Tricky one. *Bier* could mean coffin or a means of delivery to the grave. It could be a symbolic name for the tree.
16. I hope you have read C.S. Lewis's book, *That Hideous Strength*. According to Lewis, Merlin does, indeed, escape.

Until that brassy wall they up do rear:
For Merlin had in magic more insight,
Then ever him before or after living wight.

12

For he by words could call out of the sky
Both sun and moon, and make them him obey:
The land to sea, and sea to mainland dry,
And darksome night he also could turn to day:
Huge hosts of men he could alone dismay,
And hosts of men of meanest things could frame,[17]
When so him list his enemies to frighten:
That to this day for terror of his fame,
The fiends do quake, when any him to them does name.

13

And sooth,° men say that he was not the son   *in truth*
Of mortal sire, or other living wight,
But wondrously begotten, and begun
By false illusion of a guileful spirit,
On a fair lady None, that once was called
Matilda, daughter to Pubidius,
Who was the lord of Mathrauall by right,
And cousin unto king Ambrosius:
Whence he endowed was with skill so marvelous.

14

They here arriving,[18] stayed a while without,
Nor dared adventure rashly in to wander,
But of their first intent began make new doubt
For dread of danger, which it might portend:
Until the hardy maid (with love to friend)
First entering, the dreadful Mage° there found   *Magician*
Deep busied about work of wondrous end,
And writing strange characters in the ground,
With which the stubborn fiends he to his service bound.

---

17. He could turn hosts of men into horrible things, such as, say, accountants.
18. Britomart and Glauce arrived at Merlin's cave.

15

He naught was moved at their entrance bold:
For of their coming well he knew before,
Yet asked them bid their business to unfold,
As if ought in this world in secret store
Were from him hidden, or unknown of yore.
Then Glauce thus, "Let not it thee offend,
That we thus rashly through thy darksome door,
Unawares have pressed: for either fateful end,
Or other mighty cause us two did hither send."

16

He bade tell on; and then she thus began.
"Now have three moons, with borrowed brother's light,[19]
Thrice shined fair, and thrice seemed dim and wan,
Since a sore evil, which this virgin bright
Torments, and doth plunge in doleful plight,[20]
First rooting took; but what thing it might be,
Or whence it sprung, I cannot read aright:
But this I read, that but if not remedy
Thou her afford, full shortly I her dead shall see."

17

Therewith the enchanter softly began to smile
At her smooth speeches, knowing inwardly well,
That she to him disguised womanish guile,
And to her said, "Beldame,° by that you tell, *grandmother*
More need of leech-craft has your damsel,
Than of my skill: who help may have elsewhere,
In vain seeks wonders out of magic spell."[21]
The old woman grew half blank, those words to hear;
And yet was loath to let her purpose plain appear.

18

And to him said, "If any leeche's skill,
Or other learned means could have redressed

---

19. The moon only reflects (borrows) the light of the sun.
20. In other words, for three nights, Britomart has been tormented by thoughts of her beloved.
21. Prayer, maybe? Or antibiotics. Merlin's remedies would be magical, but we're in Faerie Land, remember?

This my dear daughter's deep established ill,
Certainly I should be loath thee to molest:
But this sad evil, which doth her infest,
Doth course of natural cause far exceed,
And housed is within her hollow breast,
That either seems some cursed witch's deed,
Or evil spirit that in her doth such torment breed."

19

The wizard could no longer bear her tale,
But bursting forth in laughter, to her said;
"Glauce, what needs this colorful word,
To cloak the cause, that hath itself betrayed?
Nor ye fair Britomartis, thus arrayed,
More hidden are, than sun in cloudy veil;
Whom thy good fortune, having fate obeyed,
Hath hither brought, for succor° to appeal; *assistance*
The which the powers to thee are pleased to reveal."

20

The doubtful maid, seeing herself discovered,
Was all abashed, and her pure ivory[22]
Into a clear carnation suddenly dyed;[23]
As fair Aurora rising hastily,
Doth by her blushing tell, that she did lay
All night in old Tithonus'° frozen bed, *the lover of Aurora (the dawn)*
Whereof she seems ashamed inwardly.
But her old nurse was naught disheartened,
But advantage made of that, which Merlin had aired,

21

And said, "Since then thou knowest all our grief,
(For what doest not thou know?) of grace I pray,
Pity our complaint, and yield us meet° relief." *appropriate*
With that the prophet still awhile did stay,
And then his spirit thus began forth display;

22. Skin.
23. She blushes red.

"Most noble virgin, that by fateful lore
Hast learned to love, let no whit° thee dismay   *not in the least*
The hard beginning, that meets thee in the door,
And with sharp fits thy tender heart oppresses sore.

22

"For so must all things excellent begin,
And also rooted deep must be that tree,
Whose big embodied branches shall not linger,
Till they to heaven's height forth stretched be.
For from thy womb a famous progeny
Shall spring, out of the ancient Trojan blood,
Which shall revive the sleeping memory
Of those same antique lin,° the heavens' brood,   *lineage*
Which Greece and Asian rivers stained with their blood.

23

"Renowned kings, and sacred emperors,
Thy fruitful offspring, shall from thee descend;
Brave captains, and most mighty warriors,
That shall their conquests through all lands extend,
And their decayed kingdoms shall amend:
The feeble Britons, broken with long war,
They shall uprear, and mightily defend
Against their foreign foe, that comes from far,
Till universal peace compound all civil war.

24

"It was not, Britomart, thy wandering eye,
Glancing unawares in charmed looking glass,
But the staight course of heavenly destiny,
Led with eternal providence, that has
Guided thy glance, to bring his will to pass:
Nor is thy fate, nor is thy fortune ill,
To love the bravest knight, that ever was.
Therefore submit thy ways unto his will,
And do by all due means thy destiny fulfill."

25

"But reveal," said Glauce, "thou magician
What means shall she out seek, or what ways take?
How shall she know, how shall she find the man?
Or what needs her to toil, since fates can make
Way for themselves, their purpose to partake?"
Then Merlin thus: "Indeed the fates are firm,
And may not shirk, though all the world do shake:
Yet ought men's good endeavors them confirm,
And guide the heavenly causes to their constant term.°   *fixed termination, resolution*

26

"The man whom heavens have ordained to be
The spouse of Britomart, is Artegall:
He wanders in the land of Faerie,
Yet is no Faerie borne, nor sib°   *related*
To Elves, but sprang of seed terestrial,
And formerly by false Faeries stolen away,
Whiles yet in infant cradle he did crawl;
Nor other to himself is known this day,
But that he by an Elf was gotten of a Fay.°   *a faerie*

27

"But sooth° he is the sonne of Gorlois,   *in truth*
And brother unto Cador Cornish king,
And for his warlike feats renowned is,
From where the day out of the sea doth spring,
Until the closure of the evening.
From thence, him firmly bound with faithful bond,°   *of marriage*
To this his native soil thou back shall bring,
Strongly to aid his country, to withstand
The power of foreign pagans, which invade thy land.

28

"Great aid thereto his mighty puissance,°   *power, strength*
And dreaded name shall give in that sad day:
Where also proof[24] of thy prow° valiance   *brave, loyal*

24. Remember, *proof* means "test."

Thou then shalt make, to increase thy lover's prey.
Long time ye both in arms shall bear great sway,°   *influence*
Till thy womb's burden thee from them do call,
And his last fate him from thee take away,
Too rashly cut off by practice criminal
Of secret foes, that him shall make in mischief fall.

29

"Where thee yet shall he leave for memory
Of his late puissance, his image dead,
That living, him in all activity,
To thee shall represent.[25] He from the head
Of his cousin Constantius without dread
Shall take the crown, that was his father's right,
And therewith crown himself in the other's stead:
Then shall he issue forth with dreadful might,
Against his Saxon foes in bloody field to fight.[26]

30

"Like as a lion, that in drowsy cave
Hath long time slept, himself so shall he shake,
And coming forth, shall spread his banner brave
Over the troubled south, that it shall make
The warlike Mercians[27] for fear to quake:
Thrice shall he fight with them, and twice shall win,
But the third time shall fair accordance° make: *truce*
And if he then with victory can mend,
He shall his days with peace bring to his earthly inn.°   *home*

31

"His son, hight Vortipore, shall him succeed
In kingdom, but not in felicity;°   *happiness*
Yet shall he long time war with happy speed,
And with great honor many battles try:
But at the last to the importunity

---

25. This means not a picture of the dead Artegall, but a son, who shall carry on his father's lineage and glory. In time, he will reclaim the crown from the cousin mentioned.
26. Reminder: In Britomart's time, the Saxons hadn't invaded yet. It was still Angle-land (England).
27. Southern Englanders, from Mercia.

Of froward° fortune shall be forced to yield.²⁸ *unlucky*
But his son Malgo shall full mightily
Avenge his father's loss, with spear and shield,
And his proud foes thwart in victorious field.

32

"Behold the man, and tell me Britomart,
If ever more goodly creature thou didst see;
How like a giant in each manly part
Bears he himself with portly majesty,
That one of the old Heroes seems to be:
He the six islands, of the same province²⁹
In ancient times unto great Britain,
Shall to the same reduce, and to him call
Their sundry kings to do their homage several.

33

"All which his son Careticus awhile
Shall well defend, and Saxons' power suppress,
Until a stranger king from unknown soil
Arriving, him with multitude oppress;
Great Gormond, having with huge mightiness
Ireland subdued, and therein fixed his throne,
Like a swift otter, fell through emptiness,
Shall swim over the sea with many one
Of his Norwegians, to assist the Britons' foes.³⁰

34

"He in his fury all shall overrun,
And holy Church with faithless hands deface,
That thy sad people utterly undone,
Shall to the utmost mountains fly at great pace:
Was never so great waste in any place,
Nor so foul outrage done by living men:

---

28. Lesson here: You can't win them all.
29. According to that great English historian, Geoffrey of Monmouth, at this time six countries (all islands, such as Ireland and the Orkneys) were conquered and ruled by England.
30. We're now touching on Viking lore and history. The Vikings (or Norsemen, or Danes) were constant foes. As pagans, they had no reverence for the Church and sacked the abbeys and the churches.

For all thy cities they shall sack and raze,
And the green grass, that grows, they shall burn,
That even the wild beast shall die in starved den.

35

"Whiles thus thy Britons do in languor pine,
Proud Etheldred shall from the North arise,
Serving the ambitious will of Augustine,
And passing Dee[31] with hardy enterprise,
Shall back repulse the valiant Brockwell twice,
And Bangor with massacred martyrs fill;
But the third time shall rue his foolhardiness:
For Cadwan, pitying his people's ill,
Shall stoutly him defeat, and thousand Saxons kill.

36

"But after him, Cadwallin[32] mightily
On his son Edwin[33] all those wrongs shall wreak;
Nor shall avail the wicked sorcery
Of false Pellite, his purposes to break,
But him shall slay, and on a gallows bleak
Shall give the enchanter his unhappy wage;
Then shall the Britons, late dismayed and weak,
From their long vassalage begin to be inspired,
And on their pagan foes avenge their rankled ire.

37

"Nor shall he yet his wrath so mitigate,
Till both the sons of Edwin he have slain,
Offricke and Osricke, twins unfortunate,
Both slain in battle upon Layburne plain,
Together with the king of Louthiane,°   *Scotland*
Known as Adin, and the king of Orkney,
Both joint partakers of the fatal pain:
But Penda, fearful of like destiny,
Shall yield himself his liegeman, and swear loyalty.

---

31. A river in northern England.
32. Cadwan's son, a pagan chieftain.
33. Edwin is one of our guys. Just to keep you straight.

38

"Him shall he make his fateful instrument,³⁴
To afflict the other Saxons unsubdued;
He marching forth with fury insolent
Against the good king Oswald, who endowed
With heavenly power, and by angels rescued,
All holding crosses in their hands on high,
Shall him defeat without blood imbrewd:°   *stained*
Of which, that field for endless memory,
Shall Heavenfield be called to all posterity.

39

"Where at Cadwallin's wrath shall forth issue,
And an huge host into Northumberland lead,
With which he godly Oswald shall subdue,
And crown with martyrdom his sacred head.
Whose brother Oswin, daunted with like dread,
With price of silver shall his kingdom buy,³⁵
And Penda, seeking him down to tread,
Shall tread down, and do him fouly die,³⁶
So shall with gifts his Lord Cadwallin pacify.

40

"Then shall Cadwallin die, and then the reign
Of Britons also with him at once shall die;
Nor shall the good Cadwallader³⁷ with pain,
Or power, be able it to remedy,
When the full time pre-fixed by destiny,
Shall be expired of Britons' regime.
For heaven itself shall their success envy,
And them with plagues and murrains°   *pestilent illnesses*
Consume, until all their warlike puissance be spent.

---

34. Unclear. A weapon? A document pledging his loyalty? In any case, he sided with the Britons against the Saxon invaders.
35. It was not uncommon to buy off your foes with gold and silver then.
36. Complicated, but this means Penda sought Oswin's death but instead was killed "fouly" by Oswin.
37. Cadwallin's son.

41

"Yet after all these sorrows, and huge hills
Of dying people, during eight years' space,
Cadwallader not yielding to his ills,
From Armoricke,[38] where long in wretched cache
He lived, returning to his native place,
Shall be by vision fixed in his intent:
For the heavens have decreed, to displace
The Britons, for their sins' due punishment,
And to the Saxons give over their government.

42

"Then woe, and woe, and everlasting woe,
Be to the Briton babe, that shall be born,
To live in thraldom° of his fathers foe;   *slavery*
Late king, now captive, late lord, now forlorn,
The world's reproach, the cruel victor's scorn,
Banished from princely bower to wasteland wood:
O who shall help me to lament, and mourn
The royal seed, the antique Trojan blood,
Whose empire longer here, than ever any stood."

43

The damsel[39] was full deep impassioned,
Both for his grief, and for her people's sake,
Whose future woes so plain he fashioned,
And sighing sore, at length to him thus did speak;
"Ah but will heaven's fury never slake,
Nor vengeance huge relent itself at last?
Will not long misery late mercy make,
But shall their name forever be defaced,
And quite from of the earth their memory be erased?"

44

"Nay but the term," said he, "is limited,
That in this thraldom Britons shall abide,

---

38. Armoricke is French Brittany (not a friend).
39. Britomart, of course.

CANTO III.

And the just resolution measured,
That they as strangers shall be notified.
For twice four hundred years shall be supplied,
Ere they to former rule restored shall be,
And their unfortunate fates all satisfied:
Yet during this their most obscurity,
Their beams shall oft break forth, that men them fair may see.[40]

45

"For Rhodoricke, whose surname shall be great,
Shall of himself a brave example show,
That Saxon kings his friendship shall entreat;
And Howell Dha shall goodly well endow
The savage minds with skill of justice and truth;
Then Griffyth Conan also shall uprear
His dreaded head, and the old sparks renew
Of native courage, that his foes shall fear,
Lest back again the kingdom he from them should bear.

46

"Nor shall the Saxons themselves all peaceably
Enjoy the crown, which they from Britons won
First ill, and after ruled wickedly:
For before two hundred years be full completed,
There shall a raven far from rising sun,[41]
With his wide wings upon them fiercely fly,
And bid his faithless chickens overrun[42]
The fruitful plains, and with fell cruelty,
In their vengeance, tread down the victor's insolence.

47

"Yet shall a third both these, and thine subdue;
There shall a lion from the seaboard wood
Of Neustria[43] come roaring, with a crew
Of hungry whelps, his battle-hardened bold brood,

---

40. In other words, even in the Dark Ages, light shall shine forth. (Merlin speaks of great men.)
41. The raven was the symbol of the Danes (we call them Vikings now).
42. Chickens? Sorry, guys, no clue. All I know is I'm scared of them.
43. Normandy. Spenser means William the Conqueror.

Whose claws were newly dipped in clotted blood,
That from the Danish tyrant's head shall rend
The usurped crown, as if that he were mad,
And the spoil of the country conquered
Amongst his young ones shall divide with bounty.

48

"Though when the term is full accomplished,
There shall a spark of fire, which hath long-while
Been in his ashes raked up, and hid,
Be freshly kindled in the fruitful island
Of Mona,[44] where it lurked in exile;
Which shall break forth into bright burning flame,
And reach into the house, that bears the title
Of royal majesty and sovereign name;
So shall the Briton blood their crown again reclaim.

49

"Thenceforth eternal union shall be made
Between the nations different than before,
And sacred Peace shall lovingly persuade
The warlike minds, to learn her goodly lore,
And civil wars to exercise no more:
Then shall a royal virgin reign, which shall
Stretch her white rod over the Belgic[45] shore,
And the great castle smite so sore withal,
That it shall make him shake, and shortly learn to fall.[46]

50

"But yet the end is not." There Merlin stayed,
As overcome of the spirit's power,[47]
Or other ghastly spectacle dismayed,

---

44. The historical home of the Tudor family. Henry VII, Henry VIII, and Elizabeth were Tudors.
45. Belgium, but he means all the Low Countries.
46. Spenser is talking about the Spanish control over that part of Europe (the Low Countries), which it maintained until Dutch Protestants rebelled. Elizabeth helped them by sending an army in 1585; the Spanish retaliated by sending the Spanish Armada to invade England in 1588. England won the sea battle (mainly because of a timely storm), but Spain's "Castle" and power were toppled.
47. Merlin falls into a fit, due to the power he has expended in telling this great vision to Britomart.

CANTO III.

That secretly he saw, yet not disclose:
Which sudden fit, and half ecstatic stare
When the two fearful women saw, they grew
Greatly confused in behavior;
At last the fury past, to former hue
He turned again, and cheerful looks as earlier did show.

51

Then, when themselves they well instructed had
Of all, that needed them to be inquired,
They both conceiving hope of comfort glad,
With lighter hearts unto their home retired;
Where they in secret counsel close conspired,
How to effect so hard an enterprise,[48]
And to possess the purpose they desired:
Now this, now that, between them they did devise,
And diverse plots did frame, to mask in strange disguise.

52

At last the nurse in her foolhardy wit
Conceived a bold devise,° and thus did speak;   *plan*
"Daughter, I deem that counsel ever most fit,
That of the time doth due advantage take;
Ye see that good King Uther° now doth make   *Uther, the father of Arthur*
Strong war upon the pagan brothers, called
Octa and Oza, whom he lately broke
Beside Cayr Verolame,[49] in victorious fight,
That now all Brittany doth burn in arms bright.

53

"That therefore naught our passage may impeach,
Let us in feigned arms ourselves disguise,
And our weak hands (whom need new strength shall teach)
The dreadful spear and shield to exercise:
Nor certainly, daughter, that same warlike disguise
I know, would you misbecome; for ye being tall,

---

48. They still had to find Artegall and assist him.
49. Now St. Albans.

And large of limb, to achieve an hard enterprise,
Nor anything ye want, but skill, which practice small
Will bring, and shortly make you a maid martial.°   *warlike*

54

"And sooth, it ought your courage much inflame,
To hear so often, in that royal house,
From whence to none inferior ye came,
Bards tell of many women valorous
Which have full many feats adventurous
Performed, in paragon of proudest men:
The bold Bunduca, whose victorious
Exploits made Rome to quake, stout Guendolen,
Renowned Martia, and redoubted Emmilen.

55

"And that, which more then all the rest may sway,
Late days' example, which these eyes beheld,
In the last field before Meneuia[50]
Which Uther with those foreign pagans held,
I saw a Saxon virgin, the which felled
Great Ulfin thrice upon the bloody plain,
And had not Carados her hand withheld
From rash revenge, she had him surely slain,
Yet Carados himself from her escaped with pain."

56

"Ah read," quoth Britomart, "how is she called?"
"Faire Angela," quoth she,[51] "men do her call,
No whit less fair than terrible in fight:
She hath the leading of a martial
And mighty people, dreaded more then all
The other Saxons, which do for her sake
And love, themselves of her name Angles call.
Therefore fair infant her example make
Unto thyself, and equal courage to thee take."

---

50. St. David's.
51. The nurse, Glauce.

57

Her hearty words so deep into the mind
Of the young damsel sunk, that great desire
Of warlike arms in her forthwith they fired,
And generous stout courage did inspire,
That she resolved, unknowing to her sire,
Adventurous knighthood on herself to don,
And counseled with her nurse, her maid's attire
To turned into a massy habergeon,°   *chainmail outfit*
And bade her all things put in readiness anon.°   *soon*

58

The old woman naught, that needed, did omit;
But all things did conveniently purvey:
It fortuned (so time their turn did fit)
A band of Britons riding on foray°   *riding out to battle*
Few days before, had gotten a great prey
Of Saxon goods, among the which was seen
A goodly armor, and full and richly arrayed,
Which belonged to Angela, the Saxon queen,
All fretted round with gold, and goodly well was seen.

59

The same, with all the other ornaments,
King Ryence caused to be hanged high
In his chief Church, for endless monuments
Of his success and gladful victory:
Of which herself advising readily,
In the evening late, old Glauce thither led
Fair Britomart, and that same armory
Down taking, her therein appareled,
Well as she might, and with brave baldric° garnished.   *sword belt*

60

Beside those arms there stood a mighty spear,[52]
Which Bladud made by magic art of yore,
And used the same in battle ever to bear;

---

52. Remember this spear? Guyon does.

Since which it had been here preserved in store,
For his great virtues proved long before:
For never wight so fast in saddle could sit,
But him perforce unto the ground it bore:
Both spear she took, and shield, which hung by it:
Both spear and shield of great power, for her purpose fit.

61

Thus when she had the virgin all arrayed,
Another harness, which did hang thereby,
About herself she readied, that the young maid
She might in equal arms accompany,
And as her Squire attend her carefully:
Though to their ready steeds they climbed full light,
And through back ways, that none might them espy,
Covered with secret cloud of silent night,
Themselves they forth conveyed, and passed forward right.

62

Nor rested they, till that to Faery land
They came, as Merlin them directed late:
Where meeting with this Redcross knight, she found
Of diverse things discourses to relate,
But most of Artegall, and his estate.°   *character*
At last their wayes so fell, that they must part
Then each to other well affectionate,
Friendship professed with unfeigned heart,
The Redcross knight diversed,° but forth rode Britomart.   *went another way*

CANTO III.

Word Play

Match the Spenserian words to their modern meanings.

progeny	*power*
paramour	*lover*
sooth	*test*
beldame	*related*
succor	*not in the least*
meet	*appropriate*
sib	*in truth*
puissance	*grandmother*
proof	*race, people*
whit	*assistance*

Discussion Questions

1. Merlin predicts something important will happen when Britomart and Artegall finally meet. What is it? And why, in fact, is it important?

2. What was Merlin's prophecy for peacetime?

3. What gave the old nurse, Glauce, the courage to become Britomart's squire?

Canto IV.

Bold Marinell by Britomart,
Is thrown on the rich strand:°   *shoreline*
Fair Florimell by Arthur is
Long followed, but not found.

1

Where is the antique glory now become,[1]
That whilome° used in women to appear?   *in former times*
Where be the brave achievements done by some?
Where be the battles, where the shield and spear,
And all the conquests, which them high did rear,
That matter made for famous poet's verse,
And boastful men so oft ashamed to hear?
Are they all dead, and laid in doleful hearse?
Or do they only sleep, and shall again return?

2

If they be dead, then woe is me therefore:
But if they sleep, O let them soon awake:
For all too long I burn with envy sore,
To hear the warlike feats, which Homer spoke
Of bold Penthesilea,[2] which made a lake
Of Greekish blood so oft in Trojan plain;
But when I read, how stout Debora[3] struck
Proud Sisera, and how Camille[4] hath slain
The huge Orsilochus, I swell with great disdain.[5]

---

1. Spenser longs for the warrior women of old: the queens who led their people to battle and the women who fought alongside their men. Is it, perhaps, men's insecurity that now keeps women from taking up arms?
2. He longs to hear "of bold Penthesilea," a warrior queen in *The Iliad*. She came to the aid of King Priam of Troy.
3. A judge of Israel. She battled the Canaanites, including Sisera.
4. Another warrior woman. She fought Aeneas and killed Orsilochus, the fastest man in Crete.
5. At the wimpy, whale-boned women of the sixteenth century. Oh, the vapors!

3

Yet these, and all that else had puissance,° *power, strength*
Cannot with noble Britomart compare,
As well for glory of great valiance,
As for pure chastity and virtue rare,
That all her goodly deeds do well declare.
Well worthy stock, from which the branches sprung,° *her family tree*
That in late years so fair a blossom bare,
As thee, O Queen,[6] the matter of my song,
Whose lineage from this lady I derive° along. *shall explain*

4

Who when through speeches with the Redcross knight,
She learned had the estate° of Artegall, *character*
And in each point herself informed correctly,
A friendly league of love perpetual° *undying friendship*
She with him bound, and took her leave from he.
Then he forth on his journey did proceed,[7]
To seek adventures, which might him befall,
And win him worship through his warlike deed,
Which always of his pains he made the chiefest meed.° *goal*

5

But Britomart kept on her former course,
Nor ever doffed her armor, but all the way
Grew pensive through that amorous discourse,
By which the Redcross knight did then display
Her lover's shape, and chivalrous array;° *outfit, armor*
A thousand thoughts she fashioned in her mind,
And in her feigning fancy did portray
Him such, as fittest she for love could find,
Wise, warlike, personable, courteous, and kind.[8]

---

6. Both Glorianna, the Faerie Queene, and Elizabeth I, Spenser's queen and patron.
7. Don't worry, we'll get back to his adventures.
8. Getting the idea here? She was really building him up in her mind, putting him on a pedestal. Think about the wisdom of that; don't we know that *all* have sinned and fall short of the glory of God?

6

With such self-pleasing thoughts her wound she fed,
And thought so to beguile her grievous smart;[9]
But so her smart was much more grievous bred,
And the deep wound more deep engorged her heart,
That naught but death her sorrow might depart.
So forth she rode without repose or rest,
Searching all lands and each remotest part,
Following the guidance of her blinded guest,[10]
Till that to the sea-coast at length she her addressed.°   *headed toward*

7

There she alighted from her light-foot beast,
And sitting down upon the rocky shore,
Bade her old Squire[11] unlace her lofty crest;
Though having viewed a while the sea-waves' foam,
That against the craggy cliffs did loudly roar,
And in their raging arrogance disdained,
That the fast° earth affronted them so sore,   *firm*
And their devouring covetousness restrained,
Thereat she sighed deep, and after thus complained:

8

"Huge sea of sorrow, and tempestuous grief,
Wherein my feeble bark° is tossed long,   *ship (of life)*
Far from the hoped haven of relief,
Why do thy cruel billows beat so strong,
And thy moist mountains each on others throng,°   *appear so close*
Threatening to swallow up my fearful life?
O do thy cruel wrath and spiteful wrong
At length allay, and stop thy stormy strife,
Which in these troubled bowels reigns, and rages rife.°   *much*

9

"For else my feeble vessel, crazed,° and cracked   *unsteered*
Through thy strong buffets and outrageous blows,

---

9. Pain, remember?
10. Cupid, the blind archer with really, really bad aim.
11. Glauce, her nurse in disguise.

Cannot endure, but needs it must be wrecked
On the rough rocks, or on the sandy shallows,
The while that love it steers, and fortune rows;
Love, my lewd° pilot hath a restless mind   *untrained*
And fortune bosun[12] no assurance know,
But sail without stars against tide and wind:
How can they other do, since both are bold and blind?[13]

10

"Thou god of winds, that reigns in the seas,
That reigns also in the continent,
At last blow up some gentle gale of ease,
The which may bring my ship, ere it be rent,°   *broken*
Unto the gladsome port of her° intent: *the ship's*
Then when I shall myself in safety see,
A table for eternal monument
Of thy great grace, and my great jeopardy,
Great Neptune, I avow to hallow unto thee."[14]

11

Then sighing softly sore, and inwardly deep,
She shut up all her complaint in private grief;
For her great courage would not let her weep,
Until that old Glauce began with sharp reproof,
Her to restrain, and give her good relief,
Through hope of those, which Merlin had her told
Should of her name and nation be chief,
And fetch their being from the sacred mold
Of her immortal womb, to be in heaven enrolled.[15]

12

Thus as she her comforted, she spied,
Where far away one all in armor bright,

---

12. A bosun, or "boatswain," often steers and directs the vessel.
13. Early navigation was a life-and-death affair. Before GPS, sailors relied on the stars. This extended nautical metaphor is merely saying Britomart's love is directionless. Both Love and Fortune are blind.
14. Tricky. To invent a "foundational epic" for England, Spenser pulled much from Greek and Roman mythology. When Neptune appears, it's as a character, in Spenser's intent, not as a god to be worshiped or revered as the true God.
15. Glauce reminded Britomart of Merlin's many prophecies and their happy outcomes.

With hasty gallop towards her did ride;
Her sorrow soon she ceased, and on her donned
Her helmet, to her courser° mounting light: *war horse*
Her former sorrow into sudden wrath,
Both cousin passions of a troubled spirit,
Converting, forth she beats the dusty path;
Love and disgust at once her courage kindled hath.

13

As when a foggy mist hath overcast[16]
The face of heaven, and the clear air immersed,
The world in darkness dwells, until at last
The watery south-wind from the seaboard coast
Up-blowing, doth disperse the vapor loosed,
And pours itself forth in a stormy shower;
So the fair Britomart having exchanged
Her cloudy care into a wrathful storm,
The mist of grief dissolved, did into vengeance pour.

14

The soon her goodly shield addressing fair,°   *held ready*
That mortal spear she in her hand did take,
And unto battle did herself prepare.[17]
The knight approaching, sternly her bespoke:°   *he said to her*
"Sir knight,[18] that do thy voyage rashly make
By this forbidden way in my despite,°   *in opposition of me*
Nor does by others' death example take,
I recommend thee soon retire, while thou hast might,
Lest afterward it be too late to take thy flight."

15

So thrilled with deep disdain of his proud threat,
She said this: "Fly they, that need to fly;
Words frighten babes. I mean not thee entreat°   *to ask*
To pass; but despite thee will pass or die."

16. Be patient. This is one of Spenser's ways of building suspense—a sudden epic simile.
17. Why would she assume a random knight on the beach is a foe? Well, it was a dangerous land. Skewer first and ask questions later.
18. Remember, she was dressed as a male knight.

No longer stayed for the other to reply,
But with sharp spear the rest made dearly known.
Strongly the strange knight ran, and sturdily
Struck her full on the breast, that made her down
Decline her head, and touch her saddle with her head.

16

But she again him in the shield did smite,
With so fierce fury and great puissance,
That through his triangular shield piercing quite,
And through his mailed hauberk,° by mischance   *coat of mail*
The wicked steel through his left side did glance;
Him so transfixed she before her bore
Beyond his croup,[19] the length of all her lance,
Until sadly sagging on the sandy shore,
He tumbled in an heap, and wallowed in his gore.

17

Like as the sacred ox, that careless stands,
With gilded horns, and flowery garlands crowned,
Proud of his dying honor and dear bonds,
Whiles the altars fume with frankincense around,
All suddenly with mortal stroke astounds,
Does groveling fall, and with his streaming gore
He stains the pillars, and the holy ground,
And the fair flowers, that decked him before;
So fell proud Marinell[20] upon the precious shore.

18

The martial maid stayed not him to lament,
But forward rode, and kept her ready way
Along the strand, which as she over-went,
She saw strewn all with rich array
Of pearls and precious stones of great assay,°   *value*
And all the gravel mixed with golden ore;
Whereat she wondered much, but would not stay

---

19. The force of her spear carried him off his saddle.
20. Aha! The mysterious knight is Marinell. More about him later.

For gold, or pearls, or precious stones an hour,
But them despised all; for all was in her power.

19

Whiles thus he[21] lay in deadly astonishment,
Tidings hereof came to his mother's ear;
His mother was the black-browed Cymoent,
The daughter of great Nereus, which did bear
This warlike son unto an earthly peer,°   *nobleman*
The famous mariner; who on a day
Finding the nymph asleep in secret where,°   *place*
As he by chance did wander that same way,
Was taken with her love, and by her closely lay.

20

There he this knight of her begot, whom born
She of his father Marinell did name,
And in a rocky cave as wight° forlorn,°   *creature / orphaned*
Long time she fostered up, 'til he became
A mighty man at arms, and much fame
Did get through great adventures by him done:
For never man he suffered by that same
Rich strand to travel, whereas he did wonne,°   *abide*
But that he must do battle with the sea-nymph's son.

21

An hundred knights of honorable name
He had subdued and them his vassals° made,   *servants*
That through all Faery Land his noble fame
Now blazed was, and fear did all invade,
That none dared passing through that perilous glade.
And to advance his name and glory more,
Her sea-god sire she dearly did persuade,
To endow her son with treasure and rich store,
Above all the sons, that were of earthly wombs bore.[22]

---

21. Marinell. His mother, Cymoent, is the daughter of a sea god, Nereus (one of the Titans).
22. She begged Nereus to give her son all the treasures from the sea, to make him more rich than any human.

Chastity

What does the Bible have to say about chastity? The Apostle Paul speaks directly about it, particularly in 1 Corinthians 7:1–7. For the unmarried, chastity means abstinence—refraining from sexual activity with anyone.

But some early Christians in Corinth mistook this to mean that even married people should abstain from such activity. Paul refutes them and explains God's rules:

> Now for the matters you wrote about: "It is good for a man not to have sexual relations with a woman." But since sexual immorality is occurring, each man should have sexual relations with his own wife, and each woman with her own husband. The husband should fulfill his marital duty to his wife, and likewise the wife to her husband. The wife does not have authority over her own body but yields it to her husband. In the same way, the husband does not have authority over his own body but yields it to his wife. Do not deprive each other except perhaps by mutual consent and for a time, so that you may devote yourselves to prayer. Then come together again so that Satan will not tempt you because of your lack of self-control. I say this as a concession, not as a command. I wish that all of you were as I am. But each of you has your own gift from God; one has this gift, another has that.

This, too, is chastity.

22

The god did grant his daughter's dear demand,
And to his Nephew made all riches flow;
And soon his heaped waves he did command,
Out of their hollow bosom forth to throw
All the huge treasure, which the sea below
Had in his greedy gulf devoured deep,
And him enriched through the overthrow

CANTO IV.

And wrecks of many wretches,[23] which did weep,
And often wail their wealth, which he from them did keep.

23

Shortly upon that shore there heaped was,
Exceeding riches and all precious things,
The spoil of all the world, that it did surpass
The wealth of the East, and pomp of Persian kings;
Gold, amber, ivory, pearls, brooches, rings,
And all that else was precious and dear,
The sea unto him voluntary brings,
That shortly he a great lord did appear,
As was in all the land of Faery, or elsewhere.

24

Thereto he was a brave and dreaded knight,
Tried often to the scathe of many dear,[24]
That none in equal arms him matched might,
The which his mother seeing, began to fear
Lest his too haughty hardiness might raise
Some hard mishap, in hazard of his life:
For that she oft him counseled to forbear°   *refuse*
The bloody battle, and to stir up strife,
But after all his war, to rest his weary knife.

25

And for his more assurance, she inquired
One day of Proteus[25] by his mighty spell,
(For Proteus was with prophecy inspired)
Her dear son's destiny to her to tell,
And the sad end of her sweet Marinell.
Who through foresight of his eternal skill,
Bade her from womankind to keep him well:
For of a woman he should have much ill,
A virgin strange and stout him should dismay, or kill.[26]

23. Owners who lost their ships and their cargoes.
24. His bravery was proven through many scathing injuries.
25. A sea-god who could foretell the future.
26. He warned Marinell to stay away from women. Cymoent misunderstands and thinks the threat is related to love, not chicks with swords.

26

For that she gave him warning every day,
The love of women not to entertain;
A lesson too, too hard for living clay,[27]
From love in course of nature to refrain:
Yet he his mother's lore did well retain,
And ever from fair ladies' love did fly;
Yet many ladies fair did oft complain,
That they for love of him would in all ways die:
Die, who so wished for him, he was love's enemy.

27

But ah, who can deceive his destiny,
Or ween° by warning to avoid his fate?   *think, suppose*
That when he sleeps in most security,
And safest seems, him soonest be dismayed,
And finds due effect, soon or late.
So feeble is the power of fleshly arm.
His mother bad him woman's love to hate,
For she of woman's force did fear no harm;
So weening to have armed him, she did quite disarm.[28]

28

This was that woman, this that deadly wound,
That Proteus prophesied should him dismay,
The which his mother vainly did expound,°   *explain (erroneously)*
To be heart-wounding love, which should assay°   *attempt*
To bring her son unto his last decay.
So fickle be the terms of mortal state,
And full of subtle sophisms,° which do play   *deceptions*
With double senses, and with false debate,
To approve the unknown purpose of eternal fate.

29

Too true the famous Marinell it found,
Who through late trial, on that wealthy strand

---

27. He was human, after all. Well, mostly human.
28. Like Oedipus, by trying to avoid his fate, he walked into it.

CANTO IV.

Inglorious now lies in senseless swoon,
Through heavy stroke of Britomart's hand.
Which when his mother dear did understand,
And heavy tidings heard, whereas she played
Amongst her watery sisters° by a pond,　　　　　　　　*sea nymphs*
Gathering sweet daffodils, to have made
Gay garlands, from the sun their foreheads fair to shade.²⁹

30

Yet soon both flowers and garlands far away
She flung, and her fair dewy locks she rent,°　　　　　　　*tore*
To sorrow huge she turned her former play,
And playful mirth to grievous dreariness:
She threw herself down on the continent,
No word did speak, but lay as in a swoon,
Whiles all her sisters did for her lament,
With yelling outcries, and with shrieking sound;
And every one did tear her garland from her crown.

31

Soon as she up out of her deadly fit
Arose, she bade her chariot to be brought,
And all her sisters, that with her did sit,
Bade also at once their chariots to be sought;
Though full of bitter grief and pensive thought,
She to her wagon climbed; climbed all the rest,
And forth together went, with sorrow filled.
The waves obedient to their behest,°　　　　　　　　　*command*
Them yielded ready passage, and their rage then ceased.³⁰

32

Great Neptune stood amazed at their sight,
Whiles on his broad round back they softly slid
And also himself mourned at their mournful plight,
Yet wist° not what their wailing meant, yet did　　　　　*knowing*
For great compassion of their sorrow, bid

---

29. Daffodils? What level of SPF is that, do you think?
30. The rage of the waves, not the sisters.

His mighty waters to them obedient be;
And soon the roaring billows still abated,
And all the grisly monsters of the sea
Stood gaping at their gate, and wondered them to see.

33

A team of dolphins ranged in array,
Drew the smooth chariot of sad Cymoent;
They were all taught by Triton, to obey
To the long reins, at her commandment:
As swift as swallows, on the waves they went,
That their broad flag-like fins no foam did raise,
Nor bubbling round they behind them sent;
The rest of other fishes drawn were,
Which with their finny oars the swelling sea did shear.

34

Soon as they were arrived upon the brim
Of the rich strand, their chariots they forsook,
And let their teamed fishes softly swim
Along the margins of the foamy shore,
Lest they their fins should bruise, and suffer sore
Their tender feet upon the stony ground:
And coming to the place, where all in gore
And clotted blood wallowed they found
The luckless Marinell, lying in deadly swoon;

35

His mother swooned thrice, and the third time
Could scarce recovered be out of her pain;
Had she not been devoid of mortal clay,
She should not then have been revived again,
But soon as life recovered had the rein,
She made so piteous moan and dear weeping,
That the hard rocks could scarce from tears refrain,
And all her sister nymphs with one consent
Supplied her sobbing gaps with sad complement.

36

"Dear image of myself," she said, "that is,
The wretched son of wretched mother born,
Is this thine high advancement, O is this
The immortal name, with which thee yet unborn
Thy grand-sire Nereus promised to adorn?
Now lies thou of life and honor bereft;
Now lies thou a lump of earth forlorn,
Nor of thy late life memory is left,
Nor can thy irrevocable destiny be waived?

37

"Fool Proteus, father of false prophecies,
And they more foolish, that credit to thee give,°   *those who trust you*
Not this the work of woman's hand, I know,
That so deep wound through these dear members drive.
I feared love: but they that love do live,
But they that die, do neither love nor hate.
Nevertheless, to thee thy folly I forgive,
And to myself, and to accursed fate
The guilt I do ascribe: dear wisdom bought too late.

38

"O what avails it of immortal seed[31]
To have been bred and never born to die?
Far better I it deem to die with speed,
Than waste in woe and wailing misery.
Who dies the utmost sorrow doth atone,
But who that lives, is left to wail his loss:
So life is loss, and death felicity.°   *happiness*
Sad life worse than glad death: and greater cross
To see friend's grave, than, dead, the grave self to occupy.

39

"But if the heavens did his days envy,
And my short bliss begrudge, yet might they well
Thus much afford me, ere that he did die

---

31. To have an immortal parent.

That the dim eyes of my dear Marinell
I might have closed, and him bade farewell,
Since other offices for mother meet° *appropriate*
They would not grant.
Yet despite them, farewell, my sweetest sweet;
Farewell my sweetest son, since we no more shall meet."

40

Thus when they all had sorrowed their fill,
They softly began to search his grisly wound:[32]
And that they might him handle more at will,
They him disarmed, and spreading on the ground
Their bluish mantles fringed with silver round,
They softly wiped away the clotted blood
From the orifice; which having well bound,
They poured in sovereign balm, and Nectar good,
Good both for earthly medicine, and for heavenly food.

41

Though when the lily-handed Liagore,
(This Liagore before had learned skill
In leeche's° craft, by great Apollo's lore, *doctoring*
Since her before upon high Pindus hill,[33]
He loved, and at last her womb did fill
With heavenly seed, whereof wise Pæon sprang)
Did feel his pulse, she knew there stayed still
Some little life his feeble spirit among;
Which to his mother told, despair she from her flung.

42

Though up him taking in their tender hands,
They easily unto her chariot bore:
Her team at her commandment quiet stands,
While they the corse into her wagon raise,
And strew with flowers the lamentable bier:° *bed, stretcher*
Then all the rest into their coaches climbed,
And through the brackish waves their passage shear;

32. About time!
33. A Greek mountain.

Upon great Neptune's neck they softly swim,
And to her watery chamber swiftly carry him.

43

Deep in the bottom of the sea, her bower
Is built of hollow billows heaped high,
Like to thick clouds, that threaten a stormy shower,
And vaulted all within, like to the sky,
In which the gods do dwell eternally:
There they him laid in easy couch well dressed;
And sent in haste for Tryphon, to apply
Salves to his wounds, and medicines of might:
For Tryphon of sea gods the sovereign leech is hight.°   *called*

44

Then while the nymphs sit all about him round,
Lamenting his mishap and heavy plight;
And oft his mother viewing his wide wound,
Cursed the hand, that did so deadly smite
Her dearest son, her dearest heart's delight.
But none of all those curses overtook
The warlike maid,[34] the example of that might,
But fairly well she thrived, and well did brook°   *continue*
Her noble deeds, nor her right course for aught forsook.

45

Yet did false Archimago her still pursue,[35]
To bring to pass his mischievous intent,
Now that he had her singled° from the crew   *separated*
Of courteous knights, the prince, and Faery gent,
Whom late in chase of beauty excellent
She left, pursuing that same forester strong;
Of whose foul outrage they impatient,
And full of fiery zeal, him followed long,
To rescue her from shame, and to revenge her wrong.[36]

---

34. Britomart.
35. Uh oh. Remember him from Book I? Very bad guy.
36. Remember, Arthur and Guyon ran off, pursuing a brute who was chasing a beautiful, frightened woman. Finally, we find out what happened to them!

46

Through thick and thin, through mountains and through plains,
Those two great champions did at once pursue
The fearful damsel, with incessant pains:
Who from them fled, as light-foot hare from view
Of hunter swift, and scent of hounds true.
At last they came unto a double way,
Where, doubtful which to take, her to rescue,
Themselves they did part, each to assay,
Which one more happy were, to win so goodly pray.

47

But Timias, the prince's gentle Squire,
That ladies' love unto his lord forlent,[37]
Both with proud anger, and indignant ire,
After that wicked forester fiercely went.
Had been they three, three sundry ways ybent.°   *would have taken*
But fairest fortune to the prince befell,
Whose chance it was (that soon he did repent),
To take that way, in which that damsel
Was fled before, afraid of him, as of a fiend of hell.

48

At last of her far off he gained view:
Then began he freshly prick° his foamy steed,   *spur on*
And ever as he nearer to her drew,
So evermore he did increase his speed,
And of each turning still kept wary heed:
Aloud to her he oftentimes did call,
To do away vain doubt, and needless dread:
Full mild to her he spoke, and oft let fall
Many meek words, to stay and comfort her with.

49

But nothing might relent her hasty flight;
So deep the deadly fear of that foul swain[38]

---

37. Timias gave up the love of women to better serve his prince, Arthur.
38. The forester.

Was erst° impressed in her gentle spirit: *then*
Like as a fearful dove, which through the rain,
Of the wide air her way does cut amain,°   *with great speed*
Having far off spied a bird of prey,
Which after her his nimble wings doth strain,
Doubles her haste for fear to be captured,
And with her pinions cleaves the liquid° firmament.   *clear, transparent*

50

With no less haste, and also with no less dread,
That fearful lady fled from him, that meant
To her no evil thought, nor evil deed;
Yet former fear of being foully shamed,
Carried her forward with her first intent:
And though oft looking backward, well she viewed,
Herself freed from that forester insolent,
And that it was a knight, which now her pursued,
Yet she no less the knight feared, than that villain rude.

51

His uncouth° shield and strange arms her dismayed,   *unknown*
Whose like in Faery land were seldom seen,
That fast she from him fled, no less afraid,
Than of wild beasts if she had chased been:
Yet he her followed still with courage keen,
So long that now the golden Hesperus°   *the planet Venus*
Was mounted high in top of heaven sheen,
And warned his other brethren joyous,
To light their blessed lamps in Jove's eternal house.[39]

52

All suddenly dim waxed the damp air,
And grisly shadows covered heaven bright,
That now with thousand stars was decked fair;
Which when the prince beheld, a loathsome sight,
And that being forced, for want of longer light,
He might cease his pursuit, and lose the hope

---

39. Night was falling; the stars were appearing. This is more of Spenser's *amplificatio*.

Of his long labor, he began foully wyte°   *curse, blame*
His wicked fortune, that had turned aside,
And cursed night, that robbed from him so goodly scope.°   *aim*

53

Then when her ways he could no more catch sight,
But to and fro at misadventure strayed;
Like as a ship, whose Lodestar[40] suddenly
Covered with clouds, her pilot hath dismayed;
His wearisome pursuit by force he stayed,°   *ceased*
And from his lofty steed dismounting low,
Did let him forage. Down himself he laid
Upon the grassy ground, to sleep a throw;
The cold earth was his couch, the hard steel his pillow.

54

But gentle sleep envied° him any rest;   *denied*
Instead thereof sad sorrow, and disdain
Of his hard hap did vex his noble breast,
And thousand fancies beat his idle brain
With their light wings, the sights of similarities° vain: *phantoms*
Oft did he wish, that lady fair might be
His Faery Queene, for whom he did complain:°   *sorrow for*
Or that his Faery Queene were such, as she:
And ever hasty, Night he blamed bitterly.

55

"Night thou foul mother of annoyance sad,
Sister of heavy death, and nurse of woe,
Which was begot in heaven, but for thy bad
And brutish shape thrust down to hell below,
Where by the grim flood of Cocytus[41] slow
Thy dwelling is, in Herebus' black house,
(Black Herebus thy husband is the foe
Of all the gods) where thou ungracious,[42]
Half of thy days does lead in horror hideous.

---

40. A guiding star, usually Polaris.
41. A river in Hades.
42. Specifically, *ungracious* here means "without God's grace."

56

"What had the eternal Maker need of thee,
The world in his continual course to keep,
That does all things deface, nor lets see
The beauty of His work? Indeed in sleep
The slothful body, that doth love to steep
His listless limbs, and drown his baser mind,
Doth praise thee oft, and oft from Stygian deep[43]
Calls thee, his goddess in his error blind,
And great Dame Nature's handmaid, cheering every kind.°   *living thing*

57

"But well I wote, that to an heavy heart
Thou art the root and nurse of bitter cares,
Breeder of new, renewer of old smarts:°   *wounds*
Instead of rest thou lends railing tears,
Instead of sleep, thou sends troubling fears,
And dreadful visions, in the which, alive
The dreary image of sad death appears:
So from the weary spirit thou does drive
Desired rest, and men of happiness deprive.

58

"Under thy mantle black there hidden lie,
Light-shunning theft, and traitorous intent,
Abhorred bloodshed, and vile felony,
Shameful deceit, and danger imminent;
Foul horror, and also hellish dreariness:
All these, I wote, in thy protection be,
And light does shun, for fear of being shamed:
For light alike is loathed of them and thee,[44]
And all that lewdness love, does hate the light to see.

59

"For day discovers all dishonest ways,
And shows each thing, as it is indeed:

---

43. As from the river Styx—meaning death-like.
44. Night and crime both dislike light.

The praises of high God he fair displays,
And His large bounty rightly doth decree.
Day's dearest children be the blessed seed,
Which darkness shall subdue, and heaven win;
Truth is His daughter; He her first did breed,
Most sacred virgin, without spot of sin.
Our life is day, but death with darkness doth begin.

60

"O when will day then turn to me again,
And bring with him his long expected light?
O Titan, haste to rear thy joyous wain:[45]
Speed thee to spread abroad thy beams bright?
And chase away this too long lingering night,
Chase her away, from whence she came, to hell.
She, she it is, that hath me done despite:°   *harm*
There let her with the damned spirits dwell,
And yield her room to day, that can it govern well."

61

Thus did the prince that weary night out-wear,
In restless anguish and unquiet pain:
And early, ere the morrow° did appear   *the sun*
His dewy head out of the ocean main,
He up arose, as half in great disdain,
And climbed onto his steed. So forth he went,
With heavy look and lumpish pace, that plain
In him betrayed great grudge and malcontent:
His steed also seemed to apply his steps to his intent.

---

45. The reference is to Apollo, the sun god, and his chariot.

Word Play

Match the Spenserian words to their modern meanings.

strand	*status*
whilome	*goal*
estate	*shoreline*
meed	*in former times*
array	*headed toward*
addressed	*outfit, armor*
fast	*war horse*
bark	*broken*
rent	*ship*
courser	*firm*

Discussion Questions

1. Spenser begins by lamenting the lack of strong, war-like women. Where have they gone? What reason does he propose for their absence?

2. Marinell and Florimell are both chaste—and for the same reason. What is that reason, and what is Spenser trying to tell us about Chastity with this?

3. Florimell's fear causes her to flee bad men—but also good men (Prince Arthur and his companions). Why might Spenser include this scene?

Canto V.

Prince Arthur hears of Florimell:
Three foresters Timias wounds,
Belphoebe finds him almost dead,
and rears out of swoon.

1

Wonder it is to see, in diverse minds,
How diversely love does his pageants play,
And shows his power in variable kinds:
The baser wit, whose idle thoughts always
Are wont to cleave unto the lowly clay,[1]
It stirs up to sensual desire,
And in lewd sloth to waste his careless day:
But in brave sprite it kindles goodly fire,
That to all high desert° and honor doth aspire.   *all it deserves*

2

Nor suffers it uncomely° idleness,   *unlovely*
In his free thought to build her sluggish nest:
Nor suffers it thought of ungentleness,
Ever to creep into his noble breast,
But to the highest and the worthiest
Lifts it up, that else would lowly fall:
It lets not fall, it lets it not to rest:
It lets not scarce this prince[2] to breath at all,
But to his first pursuit him forward still doth call.

3

Who long time wandered through the forest wide,

---

1. To the body and its desires.
2. Arthur.

To find some issue thence, till that at last
He met a dwarf, that seemed terrified
With some late peril, which he hardly past,
Or other accident, which him aghast;
Of whom he asked, whence he lately came,
And whither now he traveled so fast:
For sore he sweated, and running through that same
Thick forest, was scratched, and both his feet nigh lame.

4

Panting for breath, and almost out of heart,
The dwarf him answered, "Sir, ill might I stay[3]
To tell the same. I lately did depart
From Faery court, where I have many a day
Served a gentle lady of great sway,
And high accomplishment throughout all Elfin land,
Who lately left the same, and took this way:
Her now I seek, and if ye understand
Which way she fared hath, good sir tell out of hand."

5

"What mysterious wight," said he, "and how arrayed?"
"Royally clad," quoth he, "in cloth of gold,"
As meetest° may become a noble maid;   *most appropriately*
Her fair locks in rich circlet be rolled,
A fairer wight did never sun behold,
And on a palfrey° rides more white then snow,   *gentle horse*
Yet she herself is whiter much more:
The surest sign, whereby ye may her know,
Is, that she is the fairest wight alive, I vow."

6

"Now certainly, swain,"° said he, "such one I ween,   *servant*
Fast flying through this forest from her foe,
A foul, ill-favored forester, I have seen;[4]
Herself, well as I might, I rescued though,
But could not stop; so fast she did still go,

---

3. It might be dangerous . . .
4. Reminder: foresters were usually outlaws, and Spenser uses the word to mean that.

Carried away with wings of speedy fear."
"Ah dearest God," quoth he,⁵ "that is great woe,
And wondrous ruth° to all, that shall it hear.   *sorrow*
But can ye reveal sir, how I may her find, or where?"

7

"Perdy° me liefer were to weeten that,"⁶   *By God*
Said he, "than ransom of the richest knight,
Or all the good that ever yet I got:
But froward° fortune, and too forward night   *contrary*
Such happiness did, maulgre,° to me spite   *notwithstanding*
And from me robbed both life and light at once.
But dwarf, reveal, what is that lady bright,
That through this forest wanders thus alone;
For of her error strange I have great ruth° and moan."   *cause of sorrow*

8

"That lady is," quoth he, "where so she be,
The bounteous virgin, and most debonair,°   *graceful*
That ever living eye I ween did see;
Lives none this day, that may with her compare
In steadfast chastity and virtue rare,⁷
The goodly ornaments of beauty bright;
And is called Florimell the fair,
Fair Florimell beloved of many a knight,
Yet she loves none but one, that Marinell⁸ is hight.°   *called*

9

"A sea-nymph's son, that Marinell is hight,
Of my dear dame is loved dearly well;
In other none, but him, she sets delight,

---

5. The dwarf is now speaking. I know, it's tough to keep up. But think in context and it gets easier.
6. What? All right, let's break it down. *Perdy* means "truly," or more exactly, "by God" (per Deus), and *liefer* (in some texts it's spelled *lever*) means "rather." And *weeten*, a form of *weet* or *wit*, means "to know," as we all weet, right?
7. Like Shakespeare, Spenser invites us to compare characters and traits. Florimell's chastity is somewhat different from Britomart's. You don't see Britomart being chased around forests by outlaws, do you? (Yes, the armor helps.) Perhaps Florimell's is a weaker chastity, a less resolute strength in her convictions.
8. Uh oh—remember what just happened to him?

All her delight is set on Marinell;
But he sets naught at all by Florimell:
For ladies' love his mother long ago
Did him, they say, forewarn through sacred spell.
But fame now flies, that of a foreign foe
He is slain,[9] which is the ground of all our woe.

10

"Five days there be, since he," they say,[10] "was slain,
And four, since Florimell the court forsook,[11]
And vowed never to return again,
Till him alive or dead she did invent.[12]
Therefore, fair sir, for love of knighthood gent,
And honor of true ladies, if ye may
By your good counsel, or bold hardihood,
Or succor° her, or me direct the way;   *help, assist, rescue*
Do one, or other good, I you most humbly pray.

11

"So may ye gain to you full great renown,
Of all good ladies through the world so wide,
And happily in her heart find highest room,
Of whom ye seek to be most magnified:°   *praised*
At least eternal meed° shall you abide."   *reward*
To whom the prince:[13] "Dwarf, comfort to thee take,
For until thou tidings learn, what her has befallen,
I here avow thee never to forsake.
Ill wears he arms, that won't them use for ladies' sake."

12

So with the dwarf he back returned again,
To seek his lady, where he might her find;

---

9. He's not quite dead yet, remember? Still, rumor has wings, and it has been spread abroad that he was slain.
10. See, he's not sure.
11. In other words, Florimell left the Faerie Queene's court because of her love for Marinell—she had heard he was dead, or at least gravely wounded.
12. In this sense, "invent" is actually from the Latin and means "to come upon" or "discover."
13. Now Arthur is speaking again.

But by the way he greatly began complain
The want of his good squire late left behind,[14]
For whom he wondrous pensive° grew in mind, — *thoughtful, worried*
For doubt of danger, which might him betide;° — *befall*
For him he loved above all mankind,
Having him true and faithful ever tried,
And bold, as ever squire that waited by knight's side.

13

Who all this while full hard was assailed
Of deadly danger, which to him betide;° — *befall*
For whiles his lord pursued that noble maid,
After that forester foul he fiercely rid,
To been avenged of the shame, he did
To that fair damsel: him he chased long
Through the thick woods, wherein he would have hid
His shameful head from his vengeance strong,
And oft him threatened death for his outrageous wrong.

14

Nevertheless, the villain sped himself so well,
Whether through swiftness of his speedy beast,
Or knowledge of those woods, where he did dwell,
That shortly he from danger was released° — *safe from*
And out of sight escaped at the least;° — *last*
Yet not escaped from the due reward
Of his bad deeds, which daily he increased,
Nor ceased not, till him oppressed hard
The heavy plague, that for such lecherous is prepared.[15]

15

For soon as he was vanished out of sight,
His coward courage began emboldened be,
And cast to avenge him of that foul despite,° — *insult, injury*
Which he had borne of his bold enemy.
Then to his brethren came: for they were three

---

14. Remember, Timias took a different path in search of the maiden.
15. In other words, the outlaw would not escape his punishment.

Ungracious children of one graceless sire,
And unto them complained, how that he
Had used been by that foolhardy squire;
So them with bitter words he stirred to bloody ire.

16

Forthwith themselves with their sad instruments
Of spoil and murder they began to lively arm,
And with him forth into the forest went,
To wreak the wrath, which he did earnestly revive
In their stern breasts, of him which late did drive[16]
Their brother to reproach and shameful flight:
For they had vowed, that never he alive
Out of that forest should escape their might;
Vile rancor their rude hearts had filled with such spite.

17

Within that wood there was a covert glade,
Nearby a narrow ford,° to them well known,   *river crossing*
Through which it was uneasy for wight to wade;
And now by fortune it was overflowing:
By that same way they knew that Squire unknown
Might at any rate pass; for they, themselves they set
There in waiting, with thick woods overgrown,
And all the while their malice they did whet°   *sharpen*
With cruel threats, his passage through the ford to let.°   *bar*

18

It fortuned, as they devised had,
The gentle Squire came riding that same way,
Unweeting of their wile° and treason bad,   *plan*
And through the ford to pass did attempt;
But that fierce forester, which late fled away,
Stoutly forth stepping on the further shore,
Him boldly bade his passage there to stay,
Until he had made amends, and full restore
For all the damage, which he had him done before.

16. . . . which late did drive home the point.

19

With that at him a quivering dart° he threw,	*spear*
With so fell° force and villainous spite,	*mighty*
That through his hauberk° the forked head flew,	*coat of mail*
And through the linked mails it pierced quite,	
But had no power in his soft flesh to bite:	
That stroke the hardy Squire did sore displease,	
But more that him he could not come to smite;	
For by no means the high bank he could seize,	
But labored long in that deep ford with vain disease.°	*failure*

20

And still the forester with his long boar-spear	
Him kept from landing at his wished will;[17]	
And soon one[18] sent out of the thicket near	
A cruel shaft, headed with deadly ill,	
And feathered with an unlucky quill;	
The wicked steel stopped not, until it did light	
In his left thigh, and deeply did it thrill:°	*pierce*
Exceeding grief that wound in him fastened,	
But more that with his foes he could not come to chasten.[19]	

21

At last through wrath and vengeance making way,
He on the bank arrived with much pain,
Where the third brother him did sore assay,
And drove at him with all his might and main
A forest bill,[20] which both his hands did strain;
But warily he did avoid the blow,

---

17. In other words, the outlaw fended Timias off from the shore with the point of the spear.
18. One of the loathsome brothers.
19. In other words, Timias was more upset he couldn't fight his foes than he was with his wound. But here's a good time to show you what I've done with the language. The original word I substituted for "fastened" was *empight*. That wasn't even a common word when Spenser was alive. So I used a more modern meaning (the arrow was stuck deeply in Timias). But in an attempt to keep the rhyme scheme going, I substituted another word: I used "chasten," instead of the simpler word "fight" (his goal, after all, was to chastise the outlaws). My hope is to get the story—the important part—across, without slowing you down with too many words like *empight*, which force you to pause and look for a definition.
20. A pruning blade, which is nastier than it sounds. Think long pole, with sharp, curved blade at the end.

And with his spear requited° him again,   *retaliated*
That both his sides were thrilled with the throw,
And a large stream of blood out of the wound did flow.

22

He[21] tumbling down, with gnashing teeth did bite
The bitter earth, and bade to let him in
Into the baleful house of endless night,[22]
Where wicked ghosts do wail their former sin.
Though began the battle freshly to begin;
For nevermore for that spectacle bad,
Did the other two their cruel vengeance cease,
But both at once on both sides him stood,
And load upon him laid, his life for to have had.

23

Though when that villain he had seen, which late
Frightened had the fairest Florimell,
Full of fierce fury, and indignant hate,
To him he turned, and with rigor fell
Smote him so rudely on the Pannikell,°   *skull*
That to the chin he cleft his head in twain:
Down on the ground his carcass groveling fell;
His sinful soul with desperate disdain,
Out of its fleshly clay fled to the place of pain.[23]

24

That seeing now the only last of three,
Who with that wicked shaft him wounded had,
Trembling with horror, as that did foresee
The fearful end of his vengeance sad,
Through which he follow should his brethren bad,
His useless bow in feeble hand caught up,
And therewith shot an arrow at the lad;
Which faintly fluttering, scarce his helmet reached,
And glancing fell to ground, but him annoyed naught.[24]

21. One of the outlaw brothers.
22. If this isn't clear to anyone, the outlaw died.
23. Two down, one to go.
24. *Annoyed* here means "harmed." I'm sure Timias was also annoyed in the sense that we use the term.

25

With that he would have fled into the wood;
But Timias him lightly overtook,
Right as he entering was into the flood,
And struck at him with force so violent,
That headless him into the ford he sent:
The carcass with the stream was carried down,
But the head fell backward on the continent.
So mischief fell upon the meaners'° crown;   *him who meant ill*
They three be dead with shame, the squire lives with renown.

26

He lives, but takes small joy of his renown;
For of that cruel wound he bled so sore,
That from his steed he fell in deadly swoon;
Yet still the blood forth gushed in so great store,
That he lay wallowed all in his own gore.[25]
Now God thee keep, thou gentlest squire alive,
Else shall thy loving lord[26] thee see no more,
But both of comfort him thou shalt deprive,
And also thyself of honor, which thou didst achieve.

27

Providence heavenly surpasses living thought,
And doth for wretched man's relief make way;[27]
For lo, great grace or fortune thither brought
Comfort to him, that comfortless now lay.
In those same woods, ye well remember may,
How that a noble huntress[28] did wonne,°   *dwell*
She, that base Braggadochio did affray,
And made him fast out of the forest run;
Belphoebe was her name, as fair as Phoebus sun.

---

25. Told you this was a great story.
26. Spenser means Arthur.
27. In other words, God knows what we want (and need) before we know ourselves.
28. If you've not read Book II (Canto III), this is Belphoebe, one of Spenser's more intriguing characters. She's a fearless huntress who roams the forests, unafraid of outlaws, and who conquered the villainous Braggadochio of Book II. As one of the (many) symbols of Elizabeth I, she is able to both pursue battle and to heal. Think of Diana, the Roman goddess of the hunt.

28

She on a day, as she pursued the chase
Of some wild beast, which with her arrows keen
She wounded had, the same along did trace
By tract of blood, which she had freshly seen,
To have sprinkled all the grassy green;
By the great persistence, which she there perceived,
Well hoped she the beast gored had been,
And made more haste, the life to have deprived:
But ah, her expectation greatly was deceived.

29

Shortly she came, whereas that woeful squire
With blood deformed, lay in deadly swoon:
In whose fair eyes, like lamps of quenched fire,
The crystal humor[29] stood congealed round;
His locks, like faded leaves fallen to ground,
Knotted with blood, in bunches rudely ran,
And his sweet lips, on which before that stun
The bud of youth to blossom fair began,
Spoiled of their rosy red, were growing pale and wan.

30

Saw never living eye more heavy sight,
That could have made a rock of stone to rue,°   *feel sorrow*
Or rive° in twain: which when that lady bright   *split*
Besides all hope with melting eyes did view,
All suddenly ashamed, she changed hue,
And with stern horror backward began to start:
But when she better him beheld, she grew
Full of soft passion and unaccustomed pain:
The point of pity pierced through her tender heart.

31

Meekly she bowed down, to weet if life
Yet in his frozen members did remain,[30]

---

29. Their clearness.
30. The medical condition "shock" renders the body cold. So does the medical condition "dead."

And feeling by his pulses beating filled,
That the weak soul her seat did yet retain,
She cast° to comfort him with busy pain°: *rushed / effort*
His double folded neck she reared upright,
And rubbed his temples, and each trembling vein;
His mailed hauberk she did undo,
And from his head his heavy burganet° did light. *open-faced helmet*

32

Into the woods thenceforth in haste she went,
To seek for herbs, that might him remedy;
For she of herbs had great knowledge,
Taught of the nymph, which from her infancy
Her nursed had in true nobility:
There, whether it divine tobacco[31] were,
Or panacea, or polygony,[32]
She found, and brought it to her patient dear
Who all this while lay bleeding out his heart-blood near.

33

The sovereign weed° betwixt two marbles plain *plant, herb*
She pounded small, and did in pieces bruise,
And then between her lily hands twain,
Into his wound the juice thereof did squeeze,
And round about, as she could well it use,
The flesh therewith she supplied and did steep,
To abate all spasm, and soak the swelling bruise,
And after having searched the contusion deep,
She with her scarf did bind the wound from cold to keep.

34

By this he had sweet life recovered again,
And groaning inwardly deep, at last his eyes,
His watery eyes, drizzling like dewy rain,
He up began to lift toward the azure° skies, *blue*

---

31. Just say no! Tobacco, in Elizabethan times, was thought to be a healthful substance. It stopped bleeding. They didn't live long enough to get cancer; not often, anyway.
32. More healing herbs: *panacea* today means "heals all."

From whence descend all hopeless remedies:³³
Therewith he sighed, and turning him aside,
The goodly maid full of divinities,°   *divine qualities*
And gifts of heavenly grace he by him spied,
Her bow and golden quiver lying him beside.

35

"Mercy, dear lord," said he, "what grace is this,
That thou hast show to me, sinful wight,
To send thine angel from her bower of bliss,
To comfort me in my distressed plight?
Angel, or goddess do I call thee right?³⁴
What service may I do unto thee meet,°   *reciprocal*
That hast from darkness me returned to light,
And with thy heavenly salves and medicines sweet,
Hast dressed my sinful wounds? I kiss thy blessed feet."

36

Thereat she blushing said, "Ah gentle squire,
Nor goddess I, nor angel, but the maid,
And daughter of a woody nymph, desire
No service, but thy safety and aid;
Which if thou gain, I shall be well repaid.
We mortal wights, whose lives and fortunes be
To common accidents still open laid,
Are bound with common bond of frailly,
To succor° wretched wights, whom we captive see."³⁵   *assist*

37

By this her damsels,³⁶ which the former chase
Had undertaken after her, arrived,
As did Belphoebe, in the bloody place,
And thereby deemed the beast had been deprived
Of life, whom late their lady's arrow ruined:
Therefore, the bloody track they follow fast,

---

33. For divine (not only earthly) hope, we know, comes from God.
34. He asks if she is an angel or a goddess.
35. She says that man, a frail thing often in need himself, must help others as he is able.
36. Belphoebe's helpers, her hunting party.

And every one to run the swiftest strived;
But two of them the rest far were passed,
And where their lady was, arrived at the last.

38

Where when they saw that goodly boy, with blood
Defouled, and their lady dress his wounds,
They wondered much, and shortly understood,
How him in deadly case their lady found,
And rescued out of the heavy swoon.
And soon his warlike courser,° which was strayed   *warhorse*
Far in the woods, whiles that he lay in swoon,
She made those damsels search, which being delayed,
They did him set thereon, and forthwith them conveyed.

39

Into that forest far they thence him led,
Where was their dwelling, in a pleasant glade,
With mountains round about environed,
And mighty woods, which did the valley shade,
And like a stately theater it made,
Spreading itself into a spacious plain.
And in the midst a little river played
Amongst the pumice stones, which seemed complain
With gentle murmur, that his course they did restrain.

40

Beside the same a dainty place there lay,
Planted with myrtle[37] trees and laurels green,
In which the birds sung many a lovely lay
Of gods' high praise, and of their loves' sweet hurt,[38]
As it an earthly paradise had been:
In whose enclosed shadow there was pitched
A fair pavilion, scarcely to be seen,
The which was all within most richly dight,°   *decorated*
That greatest princes living it might well delight.

---

37. Myrtles were sacred to the love goddess, Venus . . . I'll let you figure out the rest.
38. What is this?

41

Thither they brought that wounded squire, and laid
In easy couch his feeble limbs to rest,
He rested him a while, and then the maid
His ready wound with better salves new dressed;
Daily she dressed him, and did the best
His grievous hurt to guarish,° that she might,   *heal*
That shortly she his sorrow hath redressed,
And his foul sore restored to fair plight:°   *bodily condition*
It she reduced,[39] but himself destroyed quite.

42

O foolish physic, and unfruitful pain,
That heals up one and makes another wound:
She his hurt thigh to him recovered again,
But hurt his heart, the which before was sound,
Through an unwary dart, which did rebound
From her fair eyes and gracious countenance.
What benefits it him from death to be unbound,
To be captive in endless endurance
Of sorrow and despair without allegiance?

43

Still as his wound did gather, and grow hole,[40]
So still his heart grew sore, and health decayed:
Madness to save a part, and lose the whole.
Still when he beheld the heavenly maid,
Whiles daily plasters to his wound she laid,
So still his malady the more increased,
The whiles her matchless beauty him dismayed.
Ah God, what other could he do at last,
But love so fair a lady, that his life released?

44

Long while he strove in his courageous breast,
With reason due the passion to subdue,

---

39. "Reduced," as in "brought low romantically." This is confusing.
40. Oooh, a Spenserian pun! While his body becomes whole (healthy), his heart grows a hole (a longing).

And love for to dislodge out of his nest:
Still when her excellencies he did view,
Her sovereign bounty, and celestial hue,
The same to love he strongly was constrained:
But when his mean[41] estate he did review,
He from such hardy boldness was restrained,
And of his luckless lot and cruel love thus complained.

45

"Unthankful wretch," said he,[42] "is this the meed,°   *reward*
With which her sovereign mercy thou doest deserve?
Thy life she saved by her gracious deed,
But thou doest ween with villainous spite,
To blot her honor, and her heavenly light.
Die, rather, die, then so disloyally
Judge of her high reward, or seem so light:
Fair death it is to shun more shame, to die:
Die rather, die, then ever love disloyally.

46

"But if to love disloyalty it be,
Shall I then hate her, that from death's door
Me brought? Ah, far be such reproach from me.
What can I less do, than her love therefore,
Since I her due reward cannot restore:
Die rather, die, and dying do her serve,
Dying her serve, and living her adore;
Thy life she gave, thy life she doth deserve:
Die rather, die, than ever from her service swerve.

47

"But foolish boy, what use thy service base
To her, to whom the heavens do serve and pursue?
Thou a mean° squire, of meek and lowly place,   *common*
She heavenly born, and of celestial hue.

---

41. Remember, Timias believed himself low-born, of "mean estate," while he viewed this lovely woman as a highly born noblewoman, way above his level.
42. He said to himself.

How then? If all love take equal view:
And doth not highest God vouchsafe to take
The love and service of the basest crew?
If she will not, die meekly for her sake;
Die, rather, die, then ever so fair love forsake."

48

Thus warred he long time against his will,
Till that through weakness he was forced at last,
To yield himself unto the mighty ill:
Which as a victor proud, began to ransack fast
His inward parts, and all his entrails waste,
That neither blood in face, nor life in heart
It left, but both did quite dry up, and blast;
As piercing lightning, which the inner part
Of everything consumes, and calcineth[43] by art.

49

Which seeing fair Belphoebe, began to fear,
Lest that his wound were inwardly well not healed,
Or that the wicked steel poisoned was:
Little she weened, that love he close concealed;[44]
Yet still he wasted, as the snow congealed,
When the bright sun his beams thereon doth beat;
Yet never he his heart to her revealed,
But rather chose to die for sorrow great,
Then with dishonorable terms[45] her to entreat.

50

She gracious lady, yet no pains did spare,
To do him ease, or do him remedy:
Many restoratives of virtues rare,
And costly cordials she did apply,
To mitigate his stubborn malady:
But that sweet cordial, which can restore

---

43. *Calcinate* means "to turn into stone."
44. She was so concerned with his physical health, she paid no attention to his heart. Smart?
45. Terms of marriage. He believed himself a commoner, remember? And she was nobility.

CANTO V.

A love-sick heart, she did to him envy;
To him, and to all the unworthy world forlorn,
She did envy that sovereign salve, in secret store.

51

That dainty rose,[46] the daughter of her morn,° *her birth*
More dear then life she tendered, whose flower
The garland of her honor did adorn:
Nor suffered she the mid-day's scorching power,
Nor the sharp northern wind thereon to shower,
But lapped up her silken leaves most tumbled down,
When so the froward sky began to lower:
But soon as calmed was the chrystal air,
She did it fair dispread, and let to flourish fair.

52

Eternal God in His almighty power,
To make example of His heavenly grace,
In paradise formerly did plant this flower,
Whence He it fetched out of her native place,
And did in stock of earthly flesh implant,
That mortal men her glory should admire
In gentle ladies' breast, and bounteous race
Of woman kind it fairest flower doth spire,
And bears fruit of honor and all chaste desire.

53

Fair imps[47] of beauty, whose bright shining beams
Adorn the world with like to heavenly light,
And to your wills both royalties and realms
Subdue, through conquest of your wondrous might,
With this fair flower your goodly garlands dressed,
Of chastity and virtue virginal,
That shall embellish more your beauty bright,
And crown your heads with heavenly coronets,
Such as the angels wear before God's tribunal.

46. Here, Spenser is talking about her virginity.
47. Offspring.

54

To your fair selves a fair example frame,
Of this fair virgin, this Belphoebe fair,
To whom in perfect love, and spotless fame,
Of chastity, none living may compare:
Nor poisonous envy justly can impair
The praise of her fresh flowering maidenhood;
Therefore, she stands on the highest stair
Of the honorable stage of womanhood,
That ladies all may follow her example long since.

55

In so great praise of steadfast chastity,
Nevertheless she was so courteous and kind,
Tempered with grace, and goodly modesty,
That seemed those two virtues strove to find
The higher place in her heroic mind:
So striving each did other more augment,
And both increased the praise of womankind,
And both increased her beauty excellent;
So all did make in her a perfect complement.

Word Play

Match the Spenserian words to their modern meanings.

desert	*unlovely*
uncomely	*sorrow*
palfrey	*deserves*
ruth	*contrary*
froward	*notwithstanding*
maulgre	*gentle horse*
magnified	*befall*
meed	*praised*
pensive	*reward*
betide	*thoughtful, worried*

Discussion Questions

1. The dwarf explains why Florimell is in the forest alone. What is her reason?

2. The squire Timias chases the villain who was chasing Florimell. What does he find? What is the outcome?

3. Timias, after being rescued by Belphoebe, falls in love with her. Instead of joy, he feels great pain and says he would rather die. Why?

Canto VI.

The birth of fair Belphoebe and
Of Amoret is told.[1]
The Gardens of Adonis fraught°   *filled*
With pleasures manifold

1

Well may I ween, fair ladies, all this while
Ye wonder, how this noble damsel[2]
So great perfections did in her compile,
Since that in savage forests she did dwell,
So far from court and royal citadel,
The great schoolmistress of all courtesy:
Seems that such wild woods should far expel
All civil usage and gentility,
And gentle spirit deform with rude rusticity.°   *rustic or uncouth ways*

2

But to this fair Belphoebe in her birth
The heavens so favorable were and free,
Looking with mild aspect upon the earth,
In the horoscope[3] of her nativity,
That all the gifts of grace and chastity
On her they poured forth of plenteous horn;[4]
Jove laughed on Venus from his sovereign seat,
And Phoebus with fair beams did her adorn,[5]
And all the Graces rocked her cradle being born.

1. Here's how this is going to go. We're going to learn about the births of both Belphoebe and her twin, Amoretta (also spelled Amoret). They represent two different kinds of chastity (and the story actually has exciting parts). As you read this, be thinking about the various aspects of this virtue.
2. Spenser means Belphoebe.
3. The planet she was born under, thought to influence one's personality and fate.
4. Remember the "Horn of Plenty," the cornucopia? That's the idea here.
5. In Spenser's PG-rated manner, he is saying that sunlight impregnated her virgin mother, Chrysogonee.

3

Her birth was of the womb of morning dew,
And her conception of the joyous Prime,[6]
And all her whole creation did her show
Pure and unspotted from all loathsome crime,[7]
That is in the genes of all fleshly slime.
So was this virgin born, so was she bred,
So was she trained up from time to time,°   *at all times*
In all chaste virtue, and true bounty
Until to her due perfection she was ripened.

4

Her mother was the fair Chrysogonee,
The daughter of Amphisa, who by race
A Faerie was, born of high degree,
She bore Belphoebe, she bore in like case
Fair Amoretta in the second place:[8]
These two were twins, and between them two did share
The heritage of all celestial grace.
That all the rest it seemed they robbed bare
Of bounty, and of beauty, and all virtues rare.

5

It were a goodly story, to declare,
By what strange accident fair Chrysogonee
Conceived these infants, and how them she bore,
In this wild forest wandering all alone,
After she had nine months fulfilled and gone:
For not as other women's common brood,
They were enwombed in the sacred throne
Of her chaste body, nor with common food,
As other women's babes, they sucked vital blood.[9]

---

6. She was born on a fine spring morning.
7. In other words, being born of a virgin, she was sinless.
8. The second twin.
9. If you are squeamish, don't read this footnote. Because their mother was a virgin, it was assumed she did not produce milk to feed them—so they nursed upon her blood instead. This is a medieval idea of physiology. Sorry.

6

But wondrously they were begot, and bred
Through influence of the heavens' fruitful ray,
As it in antique books is mentioned.
It was upon a summer's shiny day,
When Titan fair his beams did display,
In a fresh fountain, far from all men's view,
She bathed herself, the boiling heat to allay;
She bathed with roses red, and violets blue,
And all the sweetest flowers, that in the forest grew.

7

Until faint through untimely weariness, then down,
Upon the grassy ground herself she laid
To sleep, the whiles a gentle slumbering swoon
Upon her fell all naked bare displayed;
The sunbeams bright upon her body played,
Being through former bathing mollified,°   *pacified*
And pierced into her womb, where they embayed°   *awashed*
With so sweet sensation and secret power unseen,
That in her pregnant flesh they shortly fructified.°   *made fruitful, multiplied*

8

Miraculous may seem to him, that reads
So strange example of conception;
But reason teaches that the fruitful seeds
Of all things living, through impression
Of the sunbeams in moist complexion,
Do life conceive and quickened are by kind:[10]
So after Nilus'° inundation,[11]   *the Nile river*
Infinite shapes of creatures men do find,
Formed in the mud, on which the Sun hath shined.

---

10. This is a little complicated. Without going into a full explanation of the bodily humors, I'll just explain that Spenser is saying such a virgin birth is wondrous but can be explained by the fact that the sun gives life. Scholars explain this portion much better, but we're not performing scholarship here. We're reading a ripping good story.

11. The ancients believed the Nile river, along with the sun, created life, after its yearly flood.

9

Great father he[12] of generation
Is rightly called, the author of life and light;
And his fair sister for creation
Ministers matters fit,[13] which tempered right
With heat and humor, breeds the living wight.
So sprung these twins in womb of Chrysogonee,
Yet knew she naught thereof, but sore afraid,
Wondered to see her belly so blown up,
Which still increased, until she her term had full outgone.[14]

10

Whereof conceiving shame and foul disgrace,°   *fearing embarrassment*
Although her guiltless conscience her cleared,
She fled into the wilderness a space,
Until that unwieldy burden she had reared,
And shunned dishonor, which as death she feared:
Where weary of long travel, down to rest
Herself she set, and comfortably cheered;[15]
There a sad cloud of sleep her overcast,
And seized every sense with sorrow sore oppressed.[16]

11

It fortuned,° fair Venus having lost   *happened*
Her little son, the winged god of love,
Who for some light displeasure, which him crossed,
Was from her fled, as flighty as airy dove,
And left her blissful bower of joy above,
(So from her often he had fled away,
When she for ought him sharply did reprove,
And wandered in the world in strange array,
Disguised in thousand shapes, that none might him betray.)

---

12. "He" refers to the sun. Later, his "sister" is, of course, the moon.
13. The moon influences women's bodies.
14. Completed (nine months).
15. Relaxed, perhaps?
16. Here we have a scene change. We're leaving Chrysogonee for the moment, safely asleep. We're moving on to another part of the story, involving Venus and her son, Cupid.

12

Him for to seek, she left her heavenly house,
The house of goodly forms and fair aspects,
Whence all the world derives the glorious
Features of beauty, and all shapes select,
With which high God his workmanship hath decked;[17]
And searched every way, through which his wings
Had born him, or his track she might detect:
She promised kisses sweet, and sweeter things
Unto the man, that of him tidings to her brings.

13

First she him sought in court,[18] where most he used
Formerly to haunt, but there she found him not;
But many there she found, which sore accused
His falsehood, and with foul infamous blot
His cruel deeds and wicked wiles did spot:[19]
Ladies and lords she everywhere might hear
Complaining, how with his empoisoned shot
Their woeful hearts he wounded had before,
And so had left them languishing twixt hope and fear.

14

She then the cities sought from gate to gate,
And everyone did ask, did he him see;
And everyone her answered, that too late
He had him seen, and felt the cruelty
Of his sharp darts and hot artillery;
And everyone threw forth reproaches rife° *full of*
Of his mischievous deeds, and said, that he
Was the disturber of all civil° life, *peaceful*
The enemy of peace, and author of all strife.

---

17. Interesting, isn't it? Spenser, in writing an overtly Christian tale, mixes the true God in with pagan gods and goddesses. He includes these gods and goddesses in imitation of the ancients, such as Homer and Ovid, who were his models.
18. Here Spenser means the court of the Faerie Queene.
19. Jilted lovers, the lonely, those who have been victim to an unfaithful lover . . . Cupid was *not* a nice guy nor, as we see, was he very popular.

15

Then in the country she abroad him sought,
And in the rural cottages inquired,
Where also many complaints to her were brought,
How he their heedless hearts with love had fired,
And his false venom through their veins inspired;°   *injected*
And also the gentle shepherd swains, which sat
Keeping their fleecy flocks, as they were hired,
She sweetly heard complain, both how and what
Her son had to them done; yet she did smile thereat.[20]

16

But when in none of all these she him got,
She began to advise,° where else he might him hide: *to consider*
At last she her bethought, that she had not
Yet sought the savage woods and forests wide,
In which full many lovely nymphs abide,
Amongst whom might be, that he did closely lay,
Or that the love of some of them him tied:
For there, she thither set her course to apply,
To search the secret haunts of Diana's[21] company.

17

Shortly unto the wasteland woods she came,
Whereas she found the goddess with her crew,
After late chase of their bloodied game,
Sitting beside a fountain in a row,
Some of them washing with the liquid dew
From off their dainty limbs the dusty sweat,
And soil which did deform their lively hue;
Others lay shaded from the scorching heat;
The rest upon her person[22] gave attention great.

18

She having hung upon a bough on high
Her bow and painted quiver, had unlaced

---

20. She smiled at their pains?
21. Diana, the huntress.
22. Diana.

Her silver boots from her nimble thigh,
And her lanky loins ungirt, and chest unbraste,[23]
After her heat the breathing cold to taste;
Her golden locks, that late in tresses bright
Braided were for hindering of her haste,
Now loose about her shoulders hung undone,
And were with sweet Ambrosia all were sprinkled light.

19

Soon as she Venus saw behind her back,
She was ashamed to be so loose surprised,
And grew half wrathful against her damsel's slack,
That had not her thereof before advised,
But suffered her so carelessly undressed
Be overtaken. Soon her garments loose
Upgathering, to her bosom she comprised,°   *gathered to her*
Well as she might, and to the goddess rose,
Whiles all her nymphs did like a garland her enclose.

20

Goodly she began fair Cytherea[24] greet,
And shortly asked her, what cause her brought
Into that wilderness for her unsuited,
From her sweet bowers, and beds with pleasures fraught:
That sudden change, she strange adventure thought.
To whom half weeping, she thus answered,
That she her dearest son Cupid sought,
Who in his frowardness from her was fled;
That she repented sore, to have him angered.

21

Thereat Diana began to smile, in scorn
Of her vain complaint, and to her scoffing said,
"Great pity, sure, that ye be so forlorn
Of your gay son, that gives you such good aid
To your disports: ill might you been repaid."

---

23. Hot from the chase, she loosened her garments.
24. Another name for Venus.

But she[25] was more aggrieved, and replied,
"Fair sister, ill becomes it to unbraid
A doleful heart with so disdainful pride;
The like that mine, may be your pain another time.

22

"As you in woods and wanton wilderness
Your glory set, to chase the savage beasts,
So my delight is all in joyfulness,
In beds, in bowers, in banquets, and in feasts:
And ill becomes you with your lofty crests,°   *ornaments on helmets*
To scorn the joy, that Jove is glad to seek;
We both are bound to follow heaven's behests,°   *orders*
And tend our charges with obedience meek:
Spare, gentle sister, with reproach my pain to increase.

23

"And tell me, if that you my son have heard,
To lurk amongst your nymphs in secret ways;
Or keep their cabins: much I am afraid,
Lest he like one of them himself disguise,
And turn his arrows to their exercise:
So may he long himself full easy hide:
For he is fair and fresh in face and guise,°   *appearance*
As any nymph (let not it be envied)."
So saying, every nymph full narrowly she eyed.

24

But Phoebe[26] therewith sore was angered,
And sharply said: "Go, dame, go seek your boy,
Where you him lately left, in Mars' bed;
He comes not here, we scorn his foolish joy,[27]
Nor lend we leisure to his idle toy:
But if I catch him in this company,
By Stygian lake I vow, whose sad annoyance

---

25. Venus is speaking now.
26. Another name for Diana.
27. Diana's nymphs were fighters, not lovers.

The gods do dread, he dearly shall repay:
I'll clip his wanton wings, that he no more shall fly."

25

Whom when as Venus saw so sore displeased,
She inwardly sorry was, and began relent,
What she had said: so her she soon appeased,
With sugared words and gentle blandishment,[28]
Which as a fountain from her sweet lips went,
And welled goodly forth, that in short space
She[29] was well pleased, and forth her damsels sent,
Through all the woods, to search from place to place,
If any track of him or tidings they might trace.

26

To search the god of love, her nymphs she sent
Throughout the wandering forest everywhere:
And after them herself also with her went
To seek the fugitive, both far and near,
So long they sought, until they arrived were
In that same shady covert,° where lay   *secret place*
Fair Chrysogonee in slumbering trance a while:
Who in her sleep (a wondrous thing to say)
Unawares had born two babes, as fair as springing day.

27

Unawares she them conceived, unawares she bore:
She bore without pain, as she conceived
Without pleasure: nor her need implore
Lucinaes[30] aide: which when they both[31] perceived,
They were through wonder nigh of sense bereaved,°   *nearly lost their senses*
And gazing each on other, naught did speak:
At last they both agreed, her[32] seeming grieved°   *wounded, unhealthy*
Out of her heavy swoon not to awake,
But from her loving side, the tender babes to take.

28. Venus called Diana down with soft words.
29. Diana, now.
30. Juno, who aided women in labor.
31. Diana and Venus.
32. Chrysogonee.

28

Up they them took, each one a babe uptook,
And with them carried, to be fostered;
Dame Phoebe to a nymph her babe took,
To be brought up in perfect maidenhood,
And of herself, her name Belphoebe read:°   *chose*
But Venus hers thence far away conveyed,
To be brought up in goodly womanhood,[33]
And in her little love's stead, which was strayed,[34]
Her Amoretta called, to comfort her dismay.

29

She brought her to her joyous paradise,
Where most she dwells, when she on earth does dwell.
So fair a place, as Nature can devise:
Whether in Paphos, or Cytheron hill,
Or it in Gnidus[35] be, I know not well;
But well I know by trial, that this same
All other pleasant places doth excel,
And called is by her lost lover's name,
The Garden of Adonis,[36] far renowned by fame.

30

In that same Garden all the goodly flowers,
Wherewith dame Nature doth her beautify,
And decks the garlands of her paramours,°   *lovers*
Are fetched: there is the first seminary°   *a greenhouse or a seed-bed*
Of all things, that are born to live and die,
According to their kinds. Long work it were,
Here to account the endless progeny
Of all the weeds,° that bud and blossom there;   *plants*
But so much as doth need, must needs be counted here.

---

33. Maidenhood would mean a life of virginity (as Diana was a virgin); womanhood could mean eventual marriage. To Spenser, both of those are valid forms of chastity. Remember, chastity isn't the same as abstinence. Chastity means to confine sexual activity to its lawful (biblical) bounds.
34. She means, of course, Cupid.
35. Locations in Greece thought to be dear to Venus.
36. Adonis, Venus's "lost lover," was killed in a boar hunt.

31

It sited was in fruitful soil of old,
And gated in with two walls on either side;
The one of iron, the other of bright gold,
That none might through break, nor over-stride:
And double gates it had, which opened wide,
By which both in and out men might pass;
The one fair and fresh, the other old and dried:
Old Genius[37] the porter of them was,
Old Genius, the which a double nature has.

32

He lets in, he lets out to wander,
All that to come into the world desire;
A thousand thousand naked babes attend
About him day and night, which do require,
That he with fleshly weeds° would them attire: *clothing*
Such as him list,° such as eternal fate   *pleased*
Ordained hath, he clothes with sinful mire,[38]
And sends forth to live in mortal state,
Until they again return back by the hinder° gate.   *the rear gate*

33

After that they again returned been,
They in that Garden planted be again;
And grow afresh, as they had never seen
Fleshly corruption, nor mortal pain.
Some thousand years so do they there remain;
And then of him are clad with other hue,
Or sent into the changing world again,
Until thither they return, where first they grew:
So like a wheel around they run from old to new.[39]

---

37. Genius was the god of life and death.
38. Think about this one. It's unclear and hotly debated by scholars, but I think Spenser is saying the "babes" are souls waiting their births. Genius "clothes" them with the "sinful mire," or the earthly clay we are all made of, complete with original sin.
39. Is Spenser arguing for reincarnation here? Not really. He's repeating classical mythology, which—in the land of Faerie—can be considered as a sort of truth. He's not talking about our world now; he's deep in the Faerie Queene's world. One thing to think about here, perhaps, is that Spenser considers the Garden of Adonis to be a pure place, and earthly paradise. Perhaps he's saying that sin comes with birth (with the flesh) and so is impossible before birth or after death.

34

Nor needs there gardener to set, or sow,
To plant or prune: for of their own accord
All things, as they created were, do grow,
And yet remember well the mighty word,
Which first was spoken by the Almighty Lord,
That bade them to increase and multiply:[40]
Nor do they need with water of the ford,
Or of the clouds to moisten their roots dry;
For in themselves eternal moisture they apply.[41]

35

Infinite shapes of creatures there are bred,
And uncouth forms, which none yet ever knew,
And every sort is in a sundry bed
Set by itself, and ranked in comely row:
Some fit for reasoning souls to endow°   *contain*
Some made for beasts, some made for birds to wear,°   *occupy*
And all the fruitful spawn of fishes' hue°   *fleshly form*
In endless ranks along arranged were,
That seemed the ocean could not contain them there.

36

Daily they grow, and daily forth are sent
Into the world, it to replenish more;
Yet is the stock not lessened, nor spent,
But still remains in everlasting store,
As it at first created was of yore.
For in the wide womb of the world there lies,
In hateful darkness and in deep horror,
An huge eternal chaos, which supplies
The substances of Nature's fruitful progenies.[42]

37

All things from thence do their first being fetch,
And borrow matter, whereof they are made,

---

40. All right, Spenser is bringing us back to orthodox Christian beliefs now.
41. Spenser is further describing the garden. The plants and animals are self-sufficient.
42. In other words, there is endless raw material in the earth for new creatures.

 King Arthur

Who was King Arthur—if he existed at all? To the best of our knowledge, if he was real, he was a Celtic leader of a Romanized Britain in the late fifth or early sixth centuries—long after the legions had gone. He helped to defend against Saxon (Germanic) invaders. But the first confirmed mention of King Arthur wasn't until the ninth century, in a Latin text.

Most of what we think we know comes from Geoffrey of Monmouth's *Historia Regum Britanniae* (*History of the Kings of Britain*). That wasn't written until the 1130s. It was filled with as much myth and legend as actual fact.

It's from Geoffrey that we get Uther Pendragon (Arthur's father), Merlin (his wizard/advisor), most of the knights we know (Sir Kay, Sir Bedevere, Sir Gawain).

We also learn from him the story of how Arthur's nephew Mordred took both the throne and Arthur's wife, Guinevere, while Arthur was off fighting in Gaul. Arthur returned to England and defeated Mordred but received a mortal wound. He was carried off to the island of Avalon to be healed, Geoffrey tells us, and may be alive there even to this day.

Here are a few portions, from a nineteenth-century translation by J. A. Giles:

> Uther Pendragon being dead, the nobility from several provinces assembled together at Silchester, and proposed to Dubricius, archbishop of Legions, that he should consecrate Arthur, Uther's son, to be their king. For they were now in great straits, because, upon hearing of the king's death, the Saxons had invited over their countrymen from Germany, and, under the command of Colgrin, were attempting to exterminate the whole British race. They had also entirely subdued all that part of the island which extends from the Humber to the sea of Caithness. Dubricius, therefore, grieving for the calamities of his country, in conjunction with the other bishops, set the crown upon Arthur's head. Arthur was then fifteen years

old, but a youth of such unparalleled courage and generosity, joined with that sweetness of temper and innate goodness, as gained him universal love. When his coronation was over, he, according to the usual custom, showed his bounty and munificence to the people. And such a number of soldiers flocked to him upon it, that his treasury as not able to answer that vast expense. But such a spirit of generosity, joined with valour, can never long want means to support itself. Arthur, therefore, the better to keep up his munificence, resolved to make use of his courage, and to fall upon the Saxons, that he might enrich his followers with their wealth . . .

[In battle with Mordred] In this manner they spent a good part of the day, till Arthur at last made a push with his company, consisting of six thousand, six hundred and sixty-six men, against that in which he knew Mordred was; and having opened a way with their swords, they pierced quite through it, and made a grievous slaughter. For in this assault fell the wicked traitor himself, and many thousands with him. But notwithstanding the loss of him, the rest did not flee, but running together from all parts of the field maintained their ground with undaunted courage. The fight now grew more furious than ever, and proved fatal to almost all the commanders and their forces. For on Mordred's side fell Cheldric, Elasius, Egbrict, and Bunignus, Saxons; Gillapatric, Gillamor, Gistafel, and Gillarius, Irish; also the Scots and Picts, with almost all their leaders: on Arthur's side Olbrict, king of Norway; Aschillus, king of Dacia; Cador Limenic Cassibellaun, with many thousands of others, as well Britons as foreigners, that he had brought with him. And even the renowned king Arthur himself was mortally wounded; and being carried thence to the isle of Avalon to be cured of his wounds, he gave up the crown of Britain to his kinsman Constantine, the son of Cador, duke of Cornwall, in the five hundred and forty-second year of our Lord's incarnation. (*Historia Regum Britanniae* 9.1, 2)

Which when as form and feature it does take,
Becomes a body, and doth then invade
The state of life, out of the grisly shade.
That substance is eternal, and bides° so,   *remains*
Nor when the life decays, and form does fade,
Doth it consume, and into nothing go,
But changed is, and often altered to and fro.⁴³

38

The substance is not changed, nor altered,
But only the form and outward fashion;
For every substance is conditioned
To change her hue, and sundry forms to don,
Meet° for her temper and complexion: *appropriate*
For forms are variable and decay,
By course of kind, and by occasion;
And that fair flower of beauty fades away,
As doth the lily fresh before the sunny ray.

39

Great enemy to it,⁴⁴ and to all the rest,
That in the Garden of Adonis springs,
Is wicked Time, who with his scythe is dressed,⁴⁵
Does mow the flowering herbs and goodly things,
And all their glory to the ground down flings,
Where they do wither, and are foully marred:
He flies about, and with his flapping wings
Beats down both leaves and buds without regard,
Nor ever pity may relent his malice hard.

40

Yet pity often did the gods relent,
To see so fair things marred, and spoiled quite:
And their great mother Venus did lament

---

43. Spenser is arguing the conservation of mass. When the soul is gone, the body still remains.
44. To the garden.
45. Time (Chronos or Saturn) was famous for bearing a scythe, a farm implement used to harvest grain—only as Time, he harvested souls.

The loss of her dear brood, her dear delight:[46]
Her heart was pierced with pity at the sight,
When walking through the garden, them she spied,
Yet not could she find redress for such despite.°   *terrible fate*
For all that lives, is subject to that law:
All things decay in time, and to their end do draw.

41

But were it not, that Time their troubler is,
All that in this delightful garden grows,
Should happy be, and have immortal bliss:
For here all plenty, and all pleasure flows,
And sweet love gentle fits amongst them throws,
Without fell° rancor, or fond° jealousy;   *fierce / foolish*
Frankly each paramour his lover knows,
Each bird his mate, nor any does envy
Their goodly merriment, and gay felicity.

42

There is continual spring, and harvest there°   *both spring and autumn*
Continual, both meeting at one time:
For both the boughs do laughing blossoms bear,
And with fresh colors deck the wanton Prime,°   *spring*
And also at once the heavy trees they climb,
Which seem to labor under their fruits' load:
The whiles the joyous birds make their pastime
Amongst the shady leaves, their sweet abode,
And their true loves without suspicion tell abroad.[47]

43

Right in the midst of that paradise,
There stood a stately mount, on whose round top
A gloomy° grove of myrtle trees did rise,   *dense, not depressing*
Whose shady boughs sharp steel did never lop,
Nor wicked beasts their tender buds did crop,
But like a garland circled the height,

---

46. Unlike Time, which has no pity for the creatures that die, Venus does, and knows, as she wanders her garden, that all the beautiful things in it will come to their ends.
47. With their singing, the birds tell of their love.

And from their fruitful sides sweet gum did drop,
That all the ground with precious dew bedight,°   *did adorn*
Threw forth most dainty odors, and most sweet delight.

44

And in the thickest covert of that shade,
There was a pleasant arbor, not by art,
But of the trees' own inclination made,
Which knitting their rising branches part to part,
With wanton ivy vines also trailed along,
And Eglantine, and Caprifole among,
Fashioned above within their inmost part,
That nether Phoebus'° beams could through the throng,   *the sun*
Nor Aeolus'° sharp blast could work them any wrong.   *the wind*

45

And all about grew every sort of flower,
To which sad lovers were transformed of yore;[48]
Fresh Hyacinthus, Phoebus' paramour,
Foolish Narcisse, that likes the watery shore,
Sad Amaranthus, made a flower but late,[49]
Sad Amaranthus, in whose purple gore
Me seems I see Amintas' wretched fate,
To whom sweet poet's verse hath given endless date.°   *would be immortalized*

46

There used fair Venus often to enjoy
Her dear Adonis' joyous company,
And reap sweet pleasure of the wanton boy;
There yet, some say, in secret he does lay,
Lapped in flowers and precious spices,
By her hid from the world, and from the skill
Of Stygian gods, which do her love envy;[50]

---

48. Those Greek and Roman gods had a bad habit of turning their lovers into, well, interesting things—bulls, flowers, plants.
49. Hyacinth, loved by Phoebus Apollo, died and his blood was turned into the hyacinth flower. Narcissus died staring at his reflection and his body turned into a narcissus. Amaranthus is more complicated, but Spenser is probably talking about his friend, the poet Sir Philip Sidney, who had recently died of a battle wound.
50. Some said Venus hid her lover, Adonis, in that place to keep him from death.

But she herself, when ever that she will,
Possesses him, and of his sweetness takes her fill.

47

And sooth° it seems they say: for he may not — *truly*
Forever die, and ever buried be
In baleful night, where all things are forgot;
All be he subject to mortality,
Yet is eternal in mutability,° — *changeability*
And by succession made perpetual,
Transformed oft, and changed diversely:
For him the Father of all Forms[51] they call;
Therefore needs might he live, that living gives to all.

48

There now he lives in eternal bliss,
Joying his goddess, and of her enjoyed:
Nor fear he henceforth that foe of his,
Which with his cruel tusk him deadly gored:[52]
For that wild boar, the which him once annoyed,° — *gravely injured*
She firmly hath imprisoned for all time,° — *Venus locked up the boar*
That her sweet love, his malice might avoid,
In a strong rocky cave, which is they say,
Hewed underneath that mount, that none him loosen may.

49

There now he lives in everlasting joy,
With many of the gods in company,
Which thither haunt, and with the winged boy° — *Cupid*
Sporting himself in safe felicity:
Who when he hath with spoils and cruelty
Ransacked the world, and in the woeful hearts

---

51. Forms? Well, this is also a little complicated. Spenser was something of a neo-Platonist, and Platonism is a philosophy that includes the "theory of forms." That theory says the "form" of a thing is necessary to its existence. For example, I am sitting in a chair. The "form," or idea of a chair, is necessary for this chair to exist. In fact, the form is more real than the chair itself, since the form can exist without the actual chair, but the chair cannot exist without the form, or idea, of a chair. Adonis, as the "father of Forms," was a sort of creator and therefore immortal.
52. According to many versions of the myth, Adonis was killed by a wild boar.

Of many wretches set his triumphs high,
Thither resorts, and laying his sad darts
Aside, with fair Adonis plays his willful arts.

50

And his true love fair, Psyche[53] with him plays,
Fair Psyche to him lately reconciled,
After long troubles and undeserved upbraids,
With which his mother Venus her reviled,
And also himself, her cruelly exiled:
But now in steadfast love and happy state
She with him lives, and hath him borne a child,
Pleasure, that doth both gods and men gratify,
Pleasure, the daughter of Cupid and Psyche late.

51

Hither great Venus brought this infant fair,[54]
The younger daughter of Chrysogonee,
And unto Psyche with great trust and care
Committed her, fostered to be,
And trained up in true femininity:
Who no less carefully her tendered,
Than her own daughter Pleasure, to whom she
Made her companion, and her taught
In all the lore of love, and goodly womanhood.

52

In which when she to perfect ripeness grew,
Of grace and beauty noble paragon,°　　　　　　　　　　*model, ideal*
She brought her forth into the world's view,
To be the example of true love alone,
And Lodestar° of all chaste affection,　　　　　　　　　　*guide*
To all fair ladies, that do live on ground.
To Faery court she came, where many one
Admired her goodly honor, and found
His feeble heart wide lanced with love's cruel wound.

---

53. Psyche is Cupid's wife. Their daughter is Pleasure.
54. Amoretta is brought to Cupid and Psyche, and they're asked to raise her as their own.

53

But she to none of them her love did cast,
Save to the noble knight Sir Scudamour,
To whom her loving heart she linked fast
In faithful love, to abide forever more,
And for his dearest sake endured sore,
Sore trouble of an heinous enemy;
Who her would have forced to have forsaken
Her former love, and steadfast loyalty,
As ye may elsewhere read that rueful history.[55]

54

But well I ween, you first desire to learn,
What end unto that fearful damsel,
Which fled so fast from that same forester stern,
Whom with his brethren Timias slew, befell:
That was, to wit, the goodly Florimell;
Who wandering for to seek her lover dear,
Her lover dear, her dearest Marinell,
Into misfortune fell, as ye did hear,
And from Prince Arthur fled with wings of idle° fear.   *needless*

---

55. Sir Scudamour's story continues later in this book.

Match the Spenserian words to their modern meanings.

fraught	*appearance*
rusticity	*uncouth ways*
mollified	*full of*
embayed	*made fruitful*
fructified	*awashed*
fortuned	*pacified*
rife	*happened*
inspired	*to consider*
advise	*injected*
guise	*filled*

1. How was Chrysogonee impregnated? Why might Spenser, a Christian who recognizes only one virgin birth, have included this passage?

2. Was Venus moved by all the tales of the immense pain her son, Cupid, had caused? Why or why not?

3. The Garden of Adonis doesn't seem a very chaste environment, does it? How, then, do you think Amoret was brought up there as a model of chastity?

Canto VII.

The witch's son loves Florimell:
she flees, he fains° to die.   *would gladly*
Satyrane saves the Squire of Dames
from giant's tyranny.

1

Like as an hind° forth singled from the herd,   *a deer*
That has escaped from a ravenous beast,
Yet flies away of her own feet affeared,[1]
And every leaf, that shakes with the least
Murmur of wind, her terror has increased;
So fled fair Florimell from her vain[2] fear,
Long after she from peril was released:
Each shade she saw, and each noise she did hear,
Did seem to be the same, which she escaped whyleare.°   *before*

2

All that same evening she in flying spent,
And all that night her course continued:
Nor did she let dull sleep once to relent,°   *to give in*
Nor weariness to slacken her haste, but fled
Ever alike, as if her former dread
Were hard behind, her ready to arrest:°   *stop*
And her white palfrey having conquered
The mastering reins out of her weary wrest,[3]
By force her carried, wherever he thought best.

---

1. I.e., as if afraid of her own shadow (or feet).
2. Vain as in useless, not as in vanity.
3. The horse, sensing her weariness, took control and went its own way.

3

So long as breath, and able puissance °   *strength*
Did native courage unto him supply,
His pace he freshly forward did advance,
And carried her beyond all jeopardy,
But naught that wants rest, can long abide.
He having through incessant travel spent
His force, at last perforce down did lay,
Nor foot could further move: the lady gentle
Thereat was sudden struck with great astonishment.

4

And forced to alight,° on foot might always fare,° *step down / travel*
A traveler unused to such way:
Need teaches[4] her this lesson hard and rare,
That fortune all in equal balance doth sway,
And mortal miseries doth make her play.
So long she traveled, till at length she came
To an hill's side, which did to her betray°   *reveal*
A little valley, subject to the same,
All covered with thick woods, that quite it overcame.

5

Through the tops of the high trees she did descry°   *see*
A little smoke, whose vapor thin and light,
Reeking aloft, rolled up to the sky:
Which, cheerful sign did send unto her sight,
That in the same did dwell some living wight.
And soon her steps she thereunto applied,
And came at last in weary wretched plight
Unto the place, to which her hope did guide,
To find some refuge there, and rest her weary side.

6

There in a gloomy hollow glen she found
A little cottage, built of sticks and reeds
In homely ways, and walled with sods° around,   *turf*

---

4. She learns to navigate the forest on foot by need, or necessity.

In which a witch did dwell, in loathly weeds,° *clothes*
And willful want,⁵ all careless of her needs;
So choosing solitary to abide,
Far from all neighbors, that her devilish deeds
And hellish arts from people she might hide,
And hurt far off unknown, whomever she envied.

7

The damsel there arriving entered in;
Where sitting on the floor the hag she found,
Busy (as seemed) about some wicked trick:
Who soon as she beheld that sudden astonishment,
Lightly started up from the dusty ground,
And with fell look and hollow deadly gaze
Stared on her awhile, as one astounded,
Nor had one word to speak, for great amaze,
But showed by outward signs, that dread her sense did daze.

8

At last turning her fear to foolish wrath,
She asked, what devil had her thither brought,
And who she was, and what unwonted° path   *unused*
Had guided her, unwelcomed, unsought?
To which the damsel full of doubtful thought,
Her mildly answered, "Beldame° be not wrathful   *grandmother, old woman*
With silly virgin by adventure brought
Unto your dwelling, ignorant and loath,°   *unwilling*
That crave but room to rest, while tempest over blows."

9

With that down out of her crystal eyes
Few trickling tears she softly forth let fall,
That like two orient pearls, did purely shine
Upon her snowy cheek; and there with all
She sighed soft, that none so bestial,
Nor savage heart, but pity of her sad plight
Would make to melt, or piteously appall;

---

5. Willing squalor, poverty.

And that vile hag, all were her whole delight
In mischief, was much moved at so piteous sight.[6]

10

And began to comfort her in her rude° ways,	*uncouth*
With womanish compassion of her complaint,	
Wiping the tears from her suffused° eyes,	*wetted*
And bidding her sit down, to rest her faint	
And weary limbs a while. She nothing quaint°	*choosy*
Nor so disdainful of so homely° fashion,	*uncomfortable*
Since brought she was now to so hard constraint,	
Sat down upon the dusty ground anon,	
As glad of that small rest, as bird of tempest gone.°	*sheltered*

11

Though began she° gather up her garments rent,	*Florimell*
And her loose locks to dress in order due,	
With golden wreath and gorgeous ornament;	
Whom such when the wicked hag did view,	
She was astonished at her heavenly hue,°	*appearance*
And doubted her to deem an earthly wight,	
But some goddess, or of Diana's crew,	
And thought her to adore with humble spirit;	
To adore a thing so divine as beauty, were but right.	

12

This wicked woman had a wicked son,
The comfort of her age and weary days,
A lazy lord, for nothing good to have done,
But stretched forth in idleness always,
Nor ever cast his mind to covet praise,[7]
Or ply himself to any honest trade,[8]
But all the day before the sunny rays
He used to be sluggish, or sleep in slothful shade:
Such laziness both lewd and poor at once him made.[9]

---

6. In other words, even the witch took pity.
7. To seek glory, the proper (or at least usual) role of a noble knight.
8. The proper role of the commoner.
9. The sin of sloth leads to both financial and moral poverty.

13

He coming home at dinnertime, there found
The fairest creature, that he ever saw,
Sitting beside his mother on the ground;
The sight whereof did greatly him adaw,°   *overwhelm*
And his base thought with terror and with awe
So inwardly smote, that as one, which had gazed
On the bright sun unawares, does soon withdraw
His feeble eyes, with too much brightness dazed,
So stared he on her, and stood long while amazed.

14

Softly at last he began his mother ask,
What mysterious wight that was, and whence derived,
That in so strange disguise there did mask,
And by what accident she there arrived:
But she, as one nearly of her wits deprived,
With naught but ghastly looks him answered,
Like to a ghost, that lately is revived
From Stygian shores, where late it wandered;
So both at her, and each at other wondered.

15

But the fair virgin was so meek and mild,
That she to them vouchsafed to embase[10]
Her goodly deportment, and to their senses wild,
Her gentle speech applied, that in short space
She grew familiar in that deserted place.
During which time, the churl° through her so kind   *the boorish son*
And courtesy used, conceived affection base,
And cast° to love her in his brutish mind;   *planned*
No love, but brutish lust, that was so beastly tined.°   *set aflame*

16

Closely the wicked flame his bowels burned,
And shortly grew into outrageous fire;
Yet had he not the heart, nor hardiness,

---

10. In other words, she graciously promised to lower herself to their common level.

As unto her to utter his desire;
His caitiff thought dared not so high aspire,
But with soft sighs, and lovely semblances,
He weened that his affection entire
She should aread;° many resemblances   *realize on her own*
To her he made, and many kind remembrances.°   *demonstrations of love*

17

Oft from the forest wildings° he did bring,   *wild fruits*
Whose sides empurpled were with smiling red,
And oft young birds, which he had taught to sing
His mistress' praises, sweetly caroled,
Garlands of flowers sometimes for her fair head
He fine would dress; sometimes the squirrel wild
He brought to her in bands, as conquered
To be her slaves, his fellow servant wild;
All which, she from him took with countenance meek and mild.

18

But past awhile, when she fit season° saw   *time*
To leave that desert mansion, she cast[11]
In secret ways herself thence to withdraw,
For fear of mischief, which she did forecast
Might by the witch or by her son conspire:
Her weary palfrey closely, as she might,
Now well recovered after long repast,°   *rest*
In his proud furnitures° she freshly dressed,   *saddle and harness*
His late miswandered° ways now to remember right.   *wrong turns*

19

And early ere the dawning day appeared,
She forth issued, and on her journey went;
She went in peril, of each noise afraid,
And of each shade, that did itself present;
For still she feared to be overtaken,
Of that vile hag, or her uncivil son:
Who when too late awaking, well they knew,

---

11. Planned, remember?

That their fair guest was gone, they both began
To make exceeding moan, as they had been undone.

20

But that lewd lover did the most lament
For her departure, that ever man did hear;
He knocked his breast with desperate intent,
And scratched his face, and with his teeth did tear
His rugged flesh, and rent his ragged hair:
That his sad mother seeing his sore plight,
Was greatly with woe gone, and began to fear,
Lest his frail senses were perished quite,
And love to frenzy turned, since love is frantic hight.[12]

21

All ways she sought, him to restore to plight,°   *health*
With herbs, with charms, with counsel, and with tears,
But tears, nor charms, nor herbs, nor counsel might
Assuage the fury, which his entrails tears:°   *tears up his insides*
So strong is passion, that no reason hears.
Though when all other helps she saw to fail,
She turned herself back to her wicked lores
And by her devilish arts thought to prevail,
To bring her° back again, or work her final bale.°   *Florimell / death*

22

Soon out of her hidden cave she called
An hideous beast, of horrible aspect,
That could the stoutest courage have appalled;
Monstrous mishaped, and all his back was speckled
With thousand spots of colors queint elect,[13]
Thereto so swift, that it all beasts did pass:
Like never yet did living eye detect;
But like it to an hyena was,
That feeds on women's flesh, as others feed on grass.

---

12. In other words, love is known to be madness.
13. Carefully chosen.

23

It forth she called, and gave it straight the charge,
Through thick and thin her to pursue apace,
Nor once to stay to rest, or breath at large,
Until her he had attained, and brought in place,
Or quite devoured her beauty's scornful grace.
The monster swift as word, that from her went,
Went forth in haste, and did her footing trace
So sure and swiftly, through his perfect scent,
And passing speed, that shortly he her overtook.

24

Whom when the fearful damsel near he spied,
No need to bid her fast away to fly;
That ugly shape so sore her terrified,
That it she shunned no less, then dread to die,
And her fleet palfrey did so well apply
His nimble feet to her conceived fear,
That while his breath did strength to him supply,
From peril free he her away did bear:
But when his force began to fail, his pace began wax areare.°   *to slacken*

25

Which when she perceived, she was dismayed
At that same last extremity full sore,
And of her safety greatly grew afraid;
And now she began approach to the sea shore,
As it befell, that she could flee no more,
But yield herself to spoil° of greediness.   *be despoiled*
Lightly she leaped, as a wight forlorn,
From her dull horse, in desperate distress,
And to her feet betook her doubtful safeguardedness.

26

Not half so fast the wicked Myrrha[14] fled
From dread of her revenging father's hounds:

---

14. Myrrha was the mother of Adonis; she sinned with her father, unbeknownst to him, and fled his anger.

Nor half so fast to save her maidenhead,° *virginity*
Fled fearful Daphne on the Ægæan strand,[15]
As Florimell fled from that monster fierce,
To reach the sea, ere she of him were reached:
For in the sea to drown herself she fained,° *desired*
Rather than of the tyrant to be caught:
Thereto fear gave her wings, and need her courage taught.

27

It fortuned (high God did so ordain)
As she arrived on the roaring shore,
In mind to leap into the mighty main,° *sea*
A little boat lay hoving° her before, *hovering, loitering*
In which there slept a fisher old and poor,
The while his nets were drying on the sand:
Into the same she leapt, and with the oar
Did thrust the sloop from the floating strand:
So safety found at sea, which she found not at land.

28

The monster ready on the prey to seize,
Was of his forward hope deceived° quite; *deprived*
Nor dared assay° to wade the perilous seas, *brave*
But greedily long gaping at the sight,
At last in vain was forced to turn his flight,
And tell the idle tidings to his dame:
Yet to avenge his devilish spite,
He set upon her palfrey, tired lame,
And slew him cruelly, ere any rescue came.

29

And after having him disemboweled,
To fill his hellish gorge, it chanced a knight
To pass that way, as forth he traveled;
It was a goodly swain,° and of great might, *youth*
As ever man that bloody field did fight;

---

15. According to myth, Daphne was chased by Apollo, after he was shot by Cupid's arrow. She fled to preserve her virginity; she pled to a river god for help, and he turned her into the laurel tree.

But in vain shows, that wont° young knights bewitched,   *usually*
And courtly services took no delight,
But rather enjoyed to be, than seem such:
For both to be and seem to him was labor like.[16]

30

It was to weet the good Sir Satyrane,[17]
That ranged abroad to seek adventures wild,
As was his wont° in forest, and in plain;   *usual practice*
He was all armed in rugged steel unfiled,°   *unpolished*
As in the smoky forge it was compiled,
And in his scutchin° bore a satyr's head: *shield*
He coming present, where the monster wild
Upon that milk-white palfrey's carcass fed,
Unto his rescue ran, and greedily him sped.

31

There well perceived he, that it was the horse,
Whereon fair Florimell was wont to ride,
That of that fiend was ripped without remorse:
Much feared he, lest ought did ill betide
To that fair maid, the flower of women's pride;[18]
For her he dearly loved, and in all
His famous conquests highly magnified:
Besides her golden girdle,° which did fall   *belt*
From her in flight, he found, that did him sore appall.

32

Full of sad fear, and doubt-filled agony,
Fiercely he flew upon that wicked fiend,
And with huge strokes, and cruel battery
Him forced to leave his prey, for to attend
Himself from deadly danger to defend:

---

16. In other words, many young knights liked tournaments and jousts, but only that they might seem strong and brave. This knight (an old friend of ours) seemed to be and *was* both.
17. Satyrane represents the best that a natural man can be, without God's indwelling spirit. He is good, but not godly. He last appeared in Book I, Canto VI fighting Sansloy.
18. Satyrane fears that the death of Florimell's horse meant Florimell was dead, as well.

Full many wounds in his corrupted flesh
He did engrave, and much blood did spend,[19]
Yet might not do him death, but always more fresh
And fierce he still appeared, the more he did him thrash.

33

He knew not how him to despoil[20] of life,
Nor how to win the wished victory,
Since him he saw still stronger grow through strife,
And himself weaker through infirmity;
Greatly he grew enraged, and furiously
Hurling his sword away,[21] he lightly leapt
Upon the beast, that with great cruelty
Roared, and raged to be kept down:
Yet he by force him held, and strokes upon him heaped.

34

As he that strives to stop a sudden flood,
And in strong banks his violence enclose,
Forces it swell above his wonted° mood, — *usual*
And largely overflow the fruitful plain,
That all the country seems to be a main,° — *sea*
And the rich furrows° float, all quite undone: — *rows of crops*
The woeful husbandman° doth loud complain, — *farmer*
To see his whole year's labor lost so soon,
For which to God he made so many an idle boon.° — *prayer*

35

So him he held, and did through might dismay:
So long he held him, and him beat so long,
That at the last his fierceness began abate,
And meekly stoop unto the victor strong:
Who to avenge the implacable° wrong, — *irreparable*

---

19. A little help here; Satyrane "engraved" (good word) many wounds on the beast but was wounded as well (he "spent" much of his own blood). Yet each wound he gave the enchanted beast seemed to make it stronger.
20. I.e., to deprive the witch's beast of life.
21. Yeah, that was smart. Well, actually, it was, if the beast was magically protected from steel.

Which he supposed done to Florimell,
Sought by all means his sorrow to prolong,
Since dent of steel his carcass could not kill:
His maker° with her charms had formed him so well. *the witch*

36

The golden ribbon,° which that virgin wore *her belt*
About her slender waist, he took in hand,
And with it bound the beast, that loud did roar
For great spite of that unwonted band,
Yet dared not his victor to withstand,
But trembled like a lamb, fled from the prey,
And all the way him followed on the strand,
As if he had long been learned to obey;
Yet never learned he such service, until that day.

37

Thus as he led the beast along the way,
He spied far off a mighty giantess,
Fast flying on a courser dappled gray,
From a bold knight, that with great hardiness
Her hard pursued, and sought for to suppress;
She bore before her lap a doleful squire,
Lying athwart her horse in great distress,
Fast bound, hand and foot with cords of wire,
Whom she did mean to make the thrall° of her desire. *slave*

38

Which when Satyrane beheld, in haste
He left his captive beast at liberty,
And crossed the nearest way, by which he cast° *planned*
Her to encounter, ere she passed by:
But she the way shunned nevermore for that,
But forward galloped fast; which when he spied,
His mighty spear he couched warily,° *set for battle carefully*
And at her ran: she having him detected,
Herself to fight addressed, and threw her load° aside. *the poor captive squire*

39

Like as a goshawk[22], that in its foot doth bear
A trembling culver,° having spied on height   *dove, pigeon*
An Eagle, that with plumy wings doth shear
The subtle air, stooping° with all his might,   *driving*
The quarry throws to ground with deep disdain,
And to the battle doth herself prepare:
So ran the giantess unto the fight;
Her fiery eyes with furious sparks did stare,
And with blasphemous banes high God in pieces tear.[23]

40

She caught in hand an huge great iron mace,
Wherewith she many had of life deprived,
But ere the stroke could seize his aimed place,
His spear amidst her sun-broad[24] shield arrived;
Yet nevermore the steel asunder rived,°   *split*
All were the beam[25] in bigness like a mast,
Nor her out of the steadfast saddle drove,
But glancing on the tempered metal, burst
In thousand shivers, and so forth beside her past.

41

Her steed did stagger with that puissant stroke;
But she no more was moved with that might,
Then it had lighted on an aged oak;
Or on the marble pillar, that is pitched
Upon the top of Mount Olympus height,
For the brave youthful champions to assay,
With burning chariot wheels it not to smite:[26]
But who that smites it, mars his joyous play,
And is the spectacle of ruinous decay.

---

22. A type of hawk, used by hunters to capture prey.
23. With dark curses, she takes God's name in vain.
24. It was *huge*.
25. Though the spear was large.
26. In the original Olympic games, it was said young men raced chariots around a pillar on top of Olympus. They weren't allowed to touch the pillar, however (same rules apply in sailboat racing now).

42

Yet therewith sore enraged, with stern regard
Her° dreadful weapon she to him addressed,   *the giantess*
Which on his helmet martelled° so hard,   *hammered*
That made him low incline his lofty crest,
And bowed his battered visor to his breast:
Wherewith he was so stunned, that he couldn't ride,
But reeled to and fro from east to west:
Which when his cruel enemy espied,
She lightly unto him adjoined, side to side;

43

And on his collar laying puissant hand,
Out of his wavering seat him plucked by force,
By force him plucked, unable to withstand,
Or help himself, and laying athwart her horse,
In loathly way like to a carrion corpse,
She bore him fast away. Which when the knight,
That her pursued,[27] saw with great remorse,
He near was touched in his noble spirit,
And began increase his speed, as she increased her flight.

44

Whom when as near approaching she espied,
She threw away her burden angrily;
For she wished not the battle to abide,
But made herself more light, away to fly:
Yet her the hardy knight pursued so near,
That almost in the back he oft her struck:
But still when him at hand she did espy,
She turned, and semblance of fair fight did make;
But when he stayed,° to flight again she did her take.   *paused, readying to joust*

45

By this the good Sir Satyrane began wake
Out of his dream, that did him long entrance,

---

27. Remember, when we met the giantess, she had kidnapped a young squire and was being pursued by the knight who employed him. We don't know who he is yet.

And seeing none in place, he began to make
Exceeding moan, and cursed that cruel chance,
Which robbed from him so fair a chivalric deed:
At length he spied, whereas that woeful squire,
Whom he had rescued from captivity
Of his strong foe, lay tumbled in the mire,
Unable to arise, or foot or hand to stir.

46

To whom approaching, well he might perceive
In that foul plight a comely personage,
And lovely face, made fit for to deceive
Frail ladies' heart with love's consuming rage,
Now in the blossom of his freshest age:
He raised him up, and loosed his iron bands,
And after began inquire his parentage,
And how he fell into that giant's hands,
And who that was, which chased her along the lands.

47

Then trembling yet through fear, the squire did speak,[28]
"That giantess Argante is behight,°   *called*
A daughter of the Titans which did make
War against heaven, and heaped hills on height,
To scale the skies, and put Jove from his right:
Her sire Typhoeus[29] was, who mad through mirth,
And drunk with blood of men, slain by his might,
Through incest, her of his own mother Earth
Formerly begot, being but half twin of that birth.

48

"For at that birth another babe she bore,
To weet, the mighty Ollyphant,[30] that wrought
Great harm to many errant knights of yore,
And many hath to foul confusion brought.

---

28. The next section is, frankly, offensive. Feel free to skip to the start of stanza 50.
29. Also the name of a powerful wind.
30. Say it out loud.

These twins, men say, (a thing far passing thought)
Whiles in their mother's womb enclosed they were,
Ere they into the lightsome world were brought,
In fleshly lust were mingled both yfere,°   *together*
And in that monstrous way did to the world appear.

49

"So lived they ever after in like sin,
Against nature's law, and good behavior:
But greatest shame was to that maiden twin,
Who not content so foully to devour
Her native flesh, and stain her brother's bower,[31]
Did wallow in all other fleshly mire,
And suffered beasts her body to deflower:
So that she burned in that lustful fire,
Yet all that might not slake her sensual desire.

50

"But overall the country she did range,
To seek young men, to quench her flaming thirst,
And feed her fancy with delightful change:
Whom so she fittest finds to serve her lust,
Through her mighty strength, in which she most doth trust,
She with her brings into a secret isle,
Where in eternal bondage die he must,
Or be the vassal of her pleasures vile,
And in all shameful sort himself with her defile.

51

"Me, a silly wretch she so at disadvantage caught,
After she long in wait for me did lie,
And meant unto her prison to have brought,
Her loathsome pleasure there to satisfy;
That thousand deaths me liefer were to die,[32]
Then break the vow, that to fair Columbell
I plighted have, and yet keep steadfastly:

---

31. In other words, she was not yet satiated.
32. He's saying, "I would rather die a thousand deaths."

As for my name, it's no mystery to tell;
Call me the Squire of Dames, that me becomes well.

52

"But that bold knight, whom you pursuing saw
That giantess, is not such, as she seemed,
But a fair virgin, that in martial law,
And deeds of arms above all dames is deemed,
And above many knights is also esteemed,
For her great worth; she Palladine[33] is known:
She you from death, you me from dread redeemed.
Nor any may that monster match in fight,
But she, or such as she, that is so chaste a wight."

53

"Her well becomes that quest," quoth Satyrane,
"But reveal, thou Squire of Dames, what vow is this,
Which thou upon thyself have lately taken?"
"That shall I you recount," quoth he, "ywis,°   *in truth*
So be ye pleased to pardon all amiss.
That gentle lady, whom I love and serve,
After long suit and weary services,
Did ask me, how I could her love deserve,
And how she might be sure, that I would never swerve.[34]

54

"I glad by any means her grace to gain,
Bade her command my life to save, or spill.
And soon she bade me, with incessant pain
To wander through the world abroad at will,
And everywhere, where with my power or skill
I might do service unto gentle dames,
That I the same should faithfully fulfill,
And at the twelve months' end should bring their names
And pledges; as the spoils of my victorious games.[35]

---

33. She symbolizes chivalry; which Spenser relates to chastity.
34. Columbell wishes to ensure that her "Squire of Dames" will be true to her.
35. You're reading this right: She told him to go out into the world, seduce women, and bring back proof.

55

"So well I to fair ladies' service did,
And found such favor in their loving hearts,
That ere the year his course had completed,
Three hundred pledges for my good desserts,
And thrice three hundred thanks for my good parts°   *characteristics*
I with me brought, and did to her present:
Which when she saw, more inclined to add to my smarts,°   *pains*
Then to reward my trusty true intent,
She began for me devise a grievous punishment.

56

"To weet, that I my travel should resume,
And with like labor walk the world around,
Nor ever to her presence should presume,
Until I so many other dames had found,[36]
The which, for all the suit I could propound,
Would me refuse their pledges to afford,
But did abide forever chaste and sound."
"Ah gentle squire," quoth he, "tell at one word,
How many found thou such to put in thy record?"

57

"Indeed sir knight," said he, "one word may tell
All, that I ever found so wisely stayed;
For only three they were disposed so well,
And yet three years I now abroad have strayed,
To find them out." "Might I," then laughing said
The knight, "inquire of thee, what were those three,
The which thy proffered courtesies denied?
Or ill they seemed sure advised to be,
Or brutishly brought up, that never did fashions see."[37]

58

"The first which then refused me," said he
Certainly was but a common courtesan,[38]

---

36. The same number: three hundred.
37. Satyrane is saying (ironically, I believe) the Squire of Dames is so good-looking, how could women resist.
38. "Common courtesans" were prostitutes.

Yet flat refused to have to do with me,
Because I could not give her many a jane."°   *silver*
(Thereat full heartily laughed Satyrane.)
"The second was an holy nun to choose,
Which would not let me be her chaplain,°   *confessor*
Because she knew, she said, I would disclose
Her counsel, if she should her trust in me repose.

59

"The third a damsel was of low degree,
Whom I in country cottage found by chance;
Full little weened I, that chastity
Had lodging in so mean° a maintenance,°   *lowly / condition*
Yet was she fair, and in her countenance
Dwelt simple truth in seemly fashion.
Long thus I wooed her with due observance,
In hope unto my pleasure to have won;
But was as far at last, as when I first begun.

60

"Save her, I never any woman found,
That chastity did for itself embrace,
But were for other causes firm and sound;
Either for want of handsome time and place,
Or else for fear of shame and foul disgrace.
Thus am I hopeless ever to attain
My lady's love, in such a desperate case,
But all my days am like to waste in vain,
Seeking to match the chaste with the unchaste ladies in train."

61

"Perdy,"° said Satyrane, "thou Squire of Dames,   *by God*
Great labor fondly° hast thou taken in hand,   *foolishly*
To get small thanks, and therewith many blames,
That may amongst Alcides[39] labors stand."
Thence back returning to the former land,
Where late he left the beast, he overcame,

---

39. Hercules, famous for his twelve impossible labors.

He found him not; for he had broke his band,° *the golden belt*
And was returned again unto his dame,° *the witch*
To tell what tidings of fair Florimell became.

Word Play

Match the Spenserian words to their modern meanings.

fains	*overwhelm*
hind	*step down*
whyleare	*before*
alight	*would gladly*
descry	*clothes*
weeds	*deer*
loath	*see*
suffused	*unwilling*
hue	*wetted*
adaw	*appearance*

1. Florimell just can't stop running, even when her horse fails her. But she stops at a cottage. Was this a mistake? Why or why not?

2. How does Florimell's hostess react to her departure?

3. Sir Satyrane encounters a vile giantess, whose parent was the earth itself. What do you think she symbolizes?

Canto VIII.

The Witch creates a snowy lady,
Like to Florimell,
Who wrongd by churl° by Proteus saved,　　　brutish fellow
Is sought by Paridell.

1

So oft as I this history record,
My heart doth melt with pure compassion,
To think, how causeless of her own accord
This gentle damsel, whom I wrote upon,
Should plunged be in such affliction,
Without all hope of comfort or relief,
That sure I ween, the hardest heart of stone,
Would hardly find to aggravate her grief;
For misery craves rather mercy, than reproof.

2

But that accursed hag, her hostess late,
Had so rankled her malicious heart,
That she desired the abridgement of her fate,
Or long enlargement of her painful smart.[1]
Now when the beast, which by her wicked art
Late forth she sent, she back returning spied,
Tied with her broken girdle, it a part
Of her rich spoils, whom he had earlier destroyed,
She weened, and wondrous gladness to her heart applied.

3

And with it running hastily to her son,
Thought with that sight him much to have relieved;

---

1. In other words, desired her quick death or prolonged pain.

Who thereby deeming sure the thing as done,
His former grief with fury fresh revived,
Much more then earlier, and would have always rived°   *torn*
The heart out of his breast: for since her dead
He surely deemed, himself he thought deprived
Quite of all hope, wherewith he long had fed
His foolish malady, and long time had misled.[2]

4

With thought whereof, exceeding mad he grew,
And in his rage his mother would have slain,
Had she not fled into a secret mew,°   *den*
Where she was wont her spirits[3] to entertain
The masters of her art: there was she fain
To call them all in order to her aid,
And them conjure unto eternal pain,
To counsel her so carefully dismayed,
How she might heal her son, whose senses were decayed.

5

By their advice, and her own wicked wit,
She there devised a wondrous work to frame,
Whose like on earth was never formed yet,
That even Nature itself envied the same,
And grudged to see the counterfeit should shame
The thing itself. In hand she boldly took
To make another like the former dame,
Another Florimell, in shape and look
So lively and so like, that many it mistook.°   *were fooled by*

6

The substance, whereof she the body made,
Was purest snow in massive mold° congealed,   *in solid form*
Which she had gathered in a shady glade
Of the Riphoean° hills, to her revealed   *Russian*

---

2. His mother, believing the news of Florimell's death would bring her son joy, was wrong. Instead, it deepened his grief.
3. These spirits are her familiars.

By errant spirits, but from all men concealed:
The same she tempered with fine Mercury,
And virgin wax,° that never yet was sealed,   *unused sealing wax*
And mingled them with perfect vermilion,°   *a red dye*
That like a lively sanguine° it seemed to the eye.   *blood*

7

Instead of eyes, two burning lamps she set
In silver sockets, shining like the skies,
And a quick° moving spirit did assign   *living*
To stir and roll them, like a woman's eyes;
Instead of yellow locks, she did devise,
With golden wire to weave her curled head;
Yet golden wire was not so yellow thrice[4]
As Florimell's fair hair: and in the stead
Of life, she put a spirit to rule the carcass dead.

8

A wicked spirit filled with fawning guile,[5]
And fair resemblance above all the rest,
Which with the Prince of Darkness fell somewhile,°   *long ago*
From heaven's bliss and everlasting rest;
Him needed not instruct, which way were best
Himself to fashion like Florimell,
Nor how to speak, nor how to use his gestures,
For he in counterfeit did excel,
And all the wiles of women's wits knew passing° well.   *supremely*

9

Him shaped thus, she decked in garments gay,
Which Florimell had left behind her late,
That whoso then her saw, would surely say,
It was herself, whom it did imitate,
Or fairer then herself, if ought by any way
Might fairer be. And then she forth her brought
Unto her son, that lay in feeble state;

---

4. Florimell's hair was three times as golden.
5. Seemingly humble, but filled with trickery.

Who seeing her began straight start up, and thought
She was the lady self,° whom he so long had sought. *herself*

10

Though fast her clasping twixt his two arms,
Extremely joyed in so happy sight,
And soon forgot his former sickly pain;
But she, the more to seem such as she hight,[6]
Coyly rebutted his embracement light;
Yet still with gentle countenance retained,
Enough to hold a fool in vain delight:
Him long she so with shadows entertained,
As her creator had in charge to her ordained.[7]

11

Till on a day, as he disposed was
To walk the woods with that his idol fair,
Her to disport,° and idle time to pass, *divert, amuse*
In the open freshness of the gentle air,
A knight that way there chanced to repair;° *appear*
Yet knight he was not, but a boastful swain,
That deeds of arms had ever in despair,[8]
Proud Braggadocchio,[9] that in vaunting° vanity *boastful*
His glory did repose, and credit did maintain.

12

He seeing with that churl° so fair a wight, *the witch's son*
Decked with many a costly ornament,
Much marveled thereat, as well he might,
And thought that match a foul disparagement:[10]
His bloody spear soon he boldly bent° *lowered*
Against the silly° clown, who dead through fear, *simple*
Fell straight to ground in great astonishment;

---

6. To seem more like the real Florimell.
7. As the witch had carefully instructed the demon.
8. Though he was boastful, he had never won honor through noble deeds or battle.
9. From Book II, canto 3: his name says it all.
10. Braggadocchio felt the "match" (marriage or pairing) was unequal—a rude peasant with such a beautiful creature.

"Villain," said he,° "this Lady is my dear,   *Braggadocchio*
Die, if thou it gainsay:° I will away her bear."   *deny*

13

The fearful churl dared not gainsay, nor do,
But trembling stood, and yielded him the prey;
Who finding little leisure her to woo,
On Trompart's[11] steed her mounted without delay,
And without rescue led her quite away.
Proud man himself, then Braggadocchio deemed,
And next° to none, after that happy day,   *second*
Being possessed of that spoil, which seemed
The fairest wight on ground, and most of men esteemed.

14

But when he saw himself free from pursuit,[12]
He began make gentle purpose to his dame,
With terms of love and lewdness dissolute;°   *lascivious*
For he could well his glozing° speeches frame   *flattering*
To such vain uses, that him best became:
But she thereto would lend but light regard,[13]
As seeming sorry, that she ever came
Into his power, that used her so hard,
To rob her honor, which she more than life preferred.

15

Thus as they two of kindness treated° long,   *talked*
There them by chance encountered on the way
An armed knight, unto a courser strong,
Whose trampling feet unto the hollow lay°   *the ground*
Seemed to thunder, and did near affray°   *frighten*
That capon's[14] courage: yet he looked grim,
And fained° to cheer his lady in dismay,   *wished to*
Who seemed for fear to quake in every limb,
And her to save from outrage, meekly prayed° him.[15]   *begged*

11. Trompart is Braggadocchio's squire.
12. In other words, the witch's son wasn't chasing him.
13. She paid little attention.
14. A capon is a rooster; Braggadocchio was just as proud as one.
15. The false Florimell asks Braggadocchio to save her from being ravaged by the strange knight.

16

Fiercely that stranger forward came, and nigh
Approaching, with bold words and bitter threat,
Bade that same boaster, as he neared, on high°   *loudly*
To leave to him that lady for excheat,°   *as the new knight's plunder*
Or bade him battle without further treat.°   *words*
That challenge did too peremptory seem,[16]
And filled his senses with abashment° great;   *fear*
Yet seeing near him jeopardy extreme,
He it dissembled well, and light seemed to esteem.[17]

17

Saying, "Thou foolish knight, that weenst° with words   *believes*
To steal away, that I with blows have won,[18]
And brought through points of many perilous swords:
But if thee list° to see thy courser run,   *wish*
Or prove thyself, this sad encounter shun,
And seek else without hazard of thy head."
At those proud words that other knight begun
To wax° exceeding wroth, and him reared°   *grow / told*
To turn his steed about, or sure he should be dead.

18

"Since then," said Braggadocchio, "needs thou wilt[19]
Thy days abridge,° through proof of puissance,°   *shorten / might*
Turn we our steeds, that both in equal tilt°   *in a fair joust*
May meet again, and each take happy chance."
This said, they both a furlong's maintenance°   *a distance of 220 yards*
Retired their steeds, to run in even race:
But Braggadocchio with his bloody lance
Once having turned, no more returned his face,[20]
But left his love to loss, and fled himself apace.°   *swiftly*

---

16. In other words, the new knight seemed very certain, very confident.
17. He faked courage and acted as if he took the challenge lightly.
18. No he didn't!
19. In other words, "Since you wish."
20. He went to his end of the field and just kept going.

19

The knight him seeing fly, had no regard
Him to pursue, but to the lady rode,
And having her from Trompart lightly reared,[21]
Unto his courser set the lovely load,
And with her fled away without abode.°   *abiding, sticking around*
Well weened° he, that fairest Florimell   *believed*
It was, with whom in company he rode,
And so herself did always to him tell;
So made him think himself in heaven, that was in hell.[22]

20

But Florimell herself was far away,[23]
Driven to great distress by Fortune strange,
And taught the careful mariner to play,[24]
Since late mischance had her compelled to change
The land for sea, at random there to range:°   *to drift away*
Yet there that cruel Queen° avenger,   *fortune*
Not satisfied so far her to estrange°   *remove*
From courtly bliss and wonted° happiness,   *usual*
Did heap on her new waves of weary wretchedness.

21

For being fled into the fisher's boat,
For refuge from the monster's cruelty,
Long so she on the mighty main° did float,   *sea*
And with the tide drove forward carelessly;
For the air was mild, and cleared was the sky,
And all his winds Dan Aeolus° did keep,   *the god of the winds*
From stirring up their stormy enmity,
As pitying to see her wail and weep;
But all the while the fisher did securely sleep.

---

21. He also left his squire. What a guy.
22. He thought he had an angel; he, in fact, had a demon.
23. Warning: scene change. We're back to the real Florimell.
24. Remember, she escaped the witch's beast by leaping into a boat; the boatman was asleep, so she was forced to use the oars to escape the shore and the beast. That's the way she was forced ("taught") to "play" the mariner.

22

At last when drunk with drowsiness, he woke,
And saw his drover° drive along the stream, — *boat*
He was dismayed, and thrice his breast he struck,
For marvel of that accident extreme;
But when he saw that blazing beauty's beam,° — *her beaming face*
Which with rare light his boat did beautify,
He marveled more, and thought he yet did dream
Not well awake, or that some ecstasy
Besotted° had his sense, or dazed was his eye. — *dazzled*

23

But when her well avizing,° he perceived — *seeing*
To be no vision, nor fantastic sight,
Great comfort of her presence he conceived,° — *took*
And felt in his old courage new delight
To begin awake, and stir his frozen spirit,[25]
Though rudely asked her, how she thither came.
"Ah," said she, "father, I note read aright,[26]
What hard misfortune brought me to the same;
Yet am I glad that here I now in safety am.

24

"But thou good man, since far in sea we be,
And the great waters begin apace° to swell, — *quickly*
That now no more we can the mainland see,
Have care, I pray, to guide the cock-boat° well, — *small craft*
Lest worse on sea than us on land befalls."
Thereat the old man did naught but fondly° grin, — *foolishly*
And said, his boat the way could wisely tell,
But his deceitful eyes did never lin,° — *cease*
To look on her faire face, and mark° her snowy skin. — *notice*

25

The sight whereof in his congealed flesh,
Fixed such secret sting of greedy lust,

---

25. The fisherman felt old desires beginning to stir within him.
26. "I'm not sure I rightly know..."

That the dry, withered stock° it began refresh, *body*
And kindled heat, that soon in flame forth burst:
The driest wood is soonest burnt to dust.
Rudely to her he leaped, and his rough hand
Where ill became him, rashly would have thrust,
But she with angry scorn him did withstand,
And shamefully reproved for his rudeness fond.° *outlandish*

26

But he, that never good nor manners knew,
Her sharp rebuke full little did esteem;
Hard is to teach an old horse amble true.
The inward smoke, that did before but steam,
Broke into open fire and rage extreme,
And now he strength began add unto his will,
Forcing to do, that did him foul, unseemly:
Beastly he threw her down, nor cared to spoil
Her garments gay with scales of fish, that all did fill.

27

The silly° virgin strove him to withstand, *innocent*
All that she might, and him in vain reviled:
She struggled strongly both with foot and hand,
To save her honor from that villain wild,
And cried to heaven, from human help exiled.
O ye brave knights, that boast this lady's love,
Where be ye now, when she is nigh defiled
Of filthy wretch? Well may she you reprove
Of falsehood or of sloth, when most it may behoove.

28

But if that thou, Sir Satyrane, didst weet,
Or thou, Sir Peridure,° her sorry state, *a knight from Book II*
How soon would ye assemble many a fleet,
To fetch from sea, that ye at land lost late;
Towers, cities, kingdoms ye would ruin,
In your vengeance and spiteful rage,
Nor ought your burning fury might abate;

 Merlin

Remember our old friend, Geoffrey of Monmouth? *Historia Regum Britanniae* (*History of the Kings of Britain*) was not his only work. Later, he wrote a book called *Vita Merlini,* or *The Life of Merlin.*

In it, Merlin is portrayed more as a prophet than an enchanter. He is also portrayed as mad and prone to fits of fury and what we would call mental illness (this shows up in Spenser's work, as well).

Here are a few portions of *Vita Merlini,* from a 1925 translation by John Jay Parry:

> I am preparing to sing the madness of the prophetic bard, and a humorous poem on Merlin . . .
>
> Well then, after many years had passed under many kings, Merlin the Briton was held famous in the world. He was a king and prophet; to the proud people of the South Welsh he gave laws, and to the chieftains he prophesied the future . . .
>
> [After a battle in which many friends died:] He had now lamented for three whole days and had refused food, so great was the grief that consumed him. Then when he had filled the air with so many and so great complaints, new fury seized him and he departed secretly, and fled to the woods not wishing to be seen as he fled. He entered the wood and rejoiced to lie hidden under the ash trees; he marveled at the wild beasts feeding on the grass of the glades; now he chased after them and again he flew past them; he lived on the roots of grasses and on the grass, on the fruit of the trees and on the mulberries of the thicket. He became a sylvan man just as though devoted to the woods. For a whole summer after this, hidden like a wild animal, he remained buried in the woods, found by no one and forgetful of himself and of his kindred . . .
>
> [Speaking of the Saxon Wars] Uther fought them in savage battles and drove them conquered across the water with returning oars. Soon he put aside strife and re-established peace and begat a son who afterwards was so eminent that

> he was second to none in uprightness. Arthur was his name and he held the kingdom for many years after the death of his father Uther, and this he did with great grief and labour, and with the slaughter of many men in many wars. For while the aforesaid chief lay ill, from Anglia came a faithless people who with sword subdued all the country and the regions across the Humber. Arthur was a boy and on account of his youth he was not able to defeat such a force. Therefore after seeking the advice of clergy and laity he sent to Hoel, king of Brittany, and asked him to come to his aid with a swift fleet, for they were united by ties of blood and friendship, so that each was bound to relieve the distresses of the other. Hoel therefore quickly collected for the war fierce men from every side and came to us with many thousands, and joining with Arthur he attacked the enemy often, and drove them back and made terrible slaughter. With his help Arthur was secure and strong among all the troops when he attacked the enemy whom at length he conquered and forced to return to their own country, and he quieted his own kingdom by the moderation of his laws.

But if Sir Calidore could it predict,
No living creature could his cruelty assuage.

29

But since that none of all her knights is near,
See how the heavens of voluntary grace,
And sovereign favor towards chastity,
Do succor° send to her distressed case: *assistance*
So much high God doth innocence embrace.
It fortuned, while thus she stiffly° strove,   *resolutely*
And the wide sea importuned long space
With shrilling shrieks, Proteus° abroad did rove,   *a sea god*
Along the foamy waves driving his finny drove.[27]

27. Proteus was a sea-herdsman.

30

Proteus is shepherd of the seas of yore,
And hath the charge of Neptune's mighty herd;
An aged sire with head all frothy hore,°   *gray*
And sprinkled frost unto his dewy beard:
Who when those pitiful outcries he heard,
Through all the seas so ruefully resound,
His chariot swift in haste he thither steered,
Which with a team of scaly Phocas° bound   *seals*
Was drawn unto the waves, that foamed him around.

31

And coming to that fisher's wandering boat,
That went at will, without chart or sail,
He therein saw that irksome sight, which smote
Deep indignation and compassion frail°   *tender*
Into his heart at once: straight did he hail
The greedy villain from his hoped prey,
Of which he now did very little fail,[28]
And with his staff, that drives his herd astray,
Him beat so sore, that life and sense did much dismay.

32

The whiles the piteous lady up did rise,
Ruffled and foully arrayed with filthy soil,
And blubbered face with tears of her fair eyes:
Her heart near broken was with weary toil,
To save herself from that outrageous spoil,
But when she looked up, to weet, what wight
Had her from so infamous fate assoyld,°   *set free*
From shame, but more for fear of his grim sight,
Down in her lap she hid her face, and loudly shrieked.

33

Herself not saved yet from danger dread
She thought, but changed from one to other fear;
Like as a fearful partridge, that is fled

---

28. The fisherman failed in his attempt to ravage Florimell.

From the sharp hawk, which her attached near,°   *nearly seized*
And falls to ground, to seek for succor there,
Whereas the hungry spaniels she does spy,
With greedy jaws her ready for to tear;
In such distress and sad perplexity
Was Florimell, when Proteus she did see thereby.

34

But he endeavored with speeches mild
Her to comfort, and encourage bold,
Bidding her fear no more her foeman wild,
Nor doubt himself; and who he was, her told.
Yet all that could not from affright her hold,
Nor to comfort her at all prevailed;
For her faint heart was with the frozen cold
Benumbed so inwardly, that her wits nigh failed,
And all her senses with abashment° quite were quailed.°   *confusion, shame /*
    frightened

35

Her up betwixt his rugged hands he reared,
And with his frothy lips full softly kissed,
Whiles the cold icicles from his rough beard,
Dropped down unto her ivory breast:
Yet he himself so busily addressed,°   *applied himself*
That her out of astonishment he wrought,
And out of that same fisher's filthy nest
Removing her, into his chariot brought,
And there with many gentle terms her fair besought.

36

But that old lecher,° which with bold assault   *the fisherman*
That beauty dared presume to violate,
He cast° to punish for his heinous fault;   *intended*
Then took he him yet trembling since of late,
And tied behind his chariot, to gratify
The virgin, whom he had abused so sore:
So dragged him through the waves in scornful state,

And after cast him up, unto the shore;
But Florimell with him unto his bower he bore.

37

His bower is in the bottom of the main,
Under a mighty rock, against which do rave
The roaring billows in their proud disdain,
That with the angry working of the wave,
Therein is eaten out° an hollow cave,   *carved out*
That seems rough mason's[29] hand with engines keen
Had long while labored it to engrave:
There was his wonne,° nor living wight was seen,   *dwelling place*
Save one old nymph, hight° Panope to keep it clean.[30]   *called*

38

Thither he brought the sorry Florimell,
And entertained her the best he might
And Panope her entertained also well,
As an immortal might a mortal wight,
To win her liking unto his delight:
With flattering words he sweetly wooed her,
And offered fair gifts to allure her sight,
But she both offers and the offerer
Despised, and all the fawning of the flatterer.

39

Daily he tempted her with this or that,
And never suffered her to be at rest:
But evermore she him refused flat,
And all his feigned kindness did detest.
So firmly she had sealed up her breast.
Sometimes he boasted, that a god he hight,°   *was, was called*
But she a mortal creature loved best.
Then he would make himself a mortal wight;
But then she said she loved none, but a Faerie knight.[31]

---

29. Stoneworkers with great skill.
30. Maid service?
31. Remember, she fled the Faerie Court when she heard (wrongly) of Marinell's death.

40

Then like a Faerie knight himself he dressed;
For every shape on him he could endue:°   *adopt*
Then like a king he was to her expressed,
And offered kingdoms unto her in view,
To be his leman° and his lady true: *lover*
But when all this he nothing saw prevail,
With harder means he cast° her to subdue,   *contrived*
And with sharp threats her often did assail,
So thinking for to make her stubborn courage quail.

41

To dreadful shapes he did himself transform,
Now like a giant, now like to a fiend,
Then like a centaur, then like to a storm,
Raging within the waves: thereby he weened°   *thought*
Her will to win unto his wished end.
But when with fear, nor favor, nor with all
He else could do, he saw himself esteemed,°   *still rejected*
Down in a dungeon deep he let her fall,
And threatened there to make her his eternal thrall.°   *slave*

42

Eternal thralldom was to her more lief,°   *preferable*
Then loss of chastity, or change of love:
Die had she rather in tormenting grief,
Then any should of falsenesses her reprove,
Or looseness, that she lightly did remove.°   *transfer her love to another*
Most virtuous virgin, glory be thy meed,°   *reward*
And crown of heavenly praise with saints above,
Where most sweet hymns of this, thy famous deed
Are still amongst them sung, that far my rhymes exceed.[32]

43

Fit song of angels caroled to be;
But yet what so my feeble Muse can frame,

---

32. Here, Spenser is extolling Florimell's virtue. Though her chastity is *constantly* challenged, she never gives in, no matter how grave the situation. She is an example, Spenser says, for all women.

Shall be to advance thy goodly chastity,
And to enroll thy memorable name,
In the heart of every honorable dame,
That they thy virtuous deeds may imitate,
And be partakers of thy endless fame.
It irks me, leave thee in this woeful state,
To tell of Satyrane, where I him left of late,[33]

44

Who having ended with that Squire of Dames
A long discourse of his adventures vain,
The which himself, then ladies more defames,
And finding not the hyena° to be slain, *the witch's beast*
With that same squire, returned back again
To his first way.[34] And as they forward went,
They spied a knight fair pricking° on the plain, *spurring on his horse*
As if he were on some adventure bent,
And in his port° appeared manly hardiness. *manner*

45

Sir Satyrane him towards did address,
To weet, what wight he was, and what his quest:
And coming near, soon he began to guess
Both by the burning heart, which on his breast
He bore, and by the colors in his crest,
That Paridell it was. Though to him rode,
And him saluting, as seemed best,
Began first inquire of tidings far abroad;
And afterwards, on what adventures now he rode.

46

Who thereto answering, said, "The tidings bad,
Which now in Faerie court all men do tell,
Which turned hath great mirth, to mourning sad,
Is the late ruin of proud Marinell,
And sudden departure of fair Florimell,

---

33. Scene change: back to Sir Satyrane.
34. His original quest: seeking Florimell.

To find him forth: and after her are gone
All the brave knights, that do in arms excel,
To safeguard her, wandered all alone;
Amongst the rest my lot (unworthy) is to be one."[35]

47

"Ah gentle knight," said then Sir Satyrane,
"Thy labor all is lost, I greatly dread,
That hast a thankless service on thee taken,
And offer sacrifice unto the dead:
For dead, I surely doubt,° thou must accept   *fear*
Henceforth forever Florimell to be.
That all the noble knights of maidenhead,[36]
Which her adored, may sore repent with me,
And all fair ladies may forever sorry be."

48

Which words when Paridell had heard, his hue
Began greatly change, and seemed dismayed to be;
Then said, "Fair Sir, how may I ween it true,
That ye do tell in such uncertainty?
Or speak ye of report,° or did ye see   *rumor*
Just cause of dread, that makes ye doubt[37] so sore?
For perdy,° else how might it ever be,   *by God*
That ever hand should dare for to engore
Her noble blood? The heavens such cruelty abhor."[38]

49

"These eyes did see, that they will ever rue
To have seen," quoth he,° "when as a monstrous beast   *Satyrane*
The palfrey, whereon she did travel, slew,
And of his bowels made his bloody feast:
Which speaking token° showed at the least   *telling sign*
Her certain loss, if not her sure decay:

---

35. All the knights in the Faerie Court have gone in search of Florimell.
36. Spenser writes of a special Order of knights who serve Glorianna, the Faerie Queene (much like the Order of the Garter served Queen Elizabeth I).
37. Again, fear (not doubt as we think of it).
38. Paridell, sensibly, asks for proof. Did Satyrane actually see her body?

Besides, that more suspicion increased,
I found her golden girdle° cast astray,   *her belt*
Stained with dirt and blood, as relic of the prey."

50

"Aye me," said Paridell, "the signs be sad,
And but God turn the same to good soothsay,°   *omen*
That lady's safety is sore to be dreaded:
Yet will I not forsake my forward way,
Until trial do more certain truth betray."
"Fair Sir," quoth he, "well may it you succeed,
Nor long shall Satyrane behind you stay,[39]
But to the rest, which in this quest proceed
My labor add, and be partaker of their speed."

51

"Ye noble knights," said then the Squire of Dames,
"Well may ye speed in so praiseworthy pain:
But since the sun now begins to slacken his beams,
In dewy vapors of the western main,°   *sea*
And lose the team out of his weary waine,°   *wagon*
Might not mislike you[40] also to abate
Your zealous haste, till morrow next again
Both light of heaven, and strength of men relate:°   *bring back*
Which if ye please, to yonder castle turn your gate.°   *course*

52

That counsel pleased well; so all yfere°   *together*
Forth marched to a castle them before,
Where soon arriving, they restrained were
Of ready entrance, which ought evermore
To errant° knights be common: wondrous sore°   *wandering / intensely*
Thereat displeased they were, until that young squire
Began them inform the cause, why that same door
Was shut to all, which lodging did desire:
The which to let you weet, will further time require.

---

39. In other words, "I will follow you."
40. "It should not displease you."

Match the Spenserian words to their modern meanings.

churl	*living*
mew	*were fooled by*
mistook	*den*
riphoean	*divert, amuse*
sanguine	*Russian*
quick	*brutish fellow*
disport	*flattering*
gainsay	*deny*
glozing	*wish*
list	*blood*

1. The witch creates something unique to soothe her son. Describe the process and the result.

2. In an almost comedic passage, Braggadocchio gets involved. Discuss his character, and how his character brings about the results.

3. Florimell just can't win. Why does everyone seem to want to take advantage of her?

Canto IX.

Malbecco will no strange knights host,
For peevish jealousies:
Paridell jousts with Britomart:
Both show their ancestry.

1

Redoubted° knights, and honorable dames,   *respected*
To whom I level° all my labor's end,   *direct*
Right sore I fear, lest with unworthy blames
This odious argument my rhymes should shame,
Or ought your goodly patience offend,
Whiles of a wanton lady I do write,
Which with her loose inconsistency doth blend
The shining glory of your sovereign light,
And knighthood foul defaced by a faithless knight.[1]

2

But never let the example of the bad
Offend the good: for good by comparison
Of evil, may more notably be read,°   *revealed*
As white seems fair, matched with black as one;
Nor all are shamed by the fault of one;
For lo in heaven, whereas all goodness is,
Amongst the angels, a whole legion
Of wicked spirits did fall from happy bliss;
What wonder then, if one of women all did amiss?

---

1. Spenser starts this Canto with an apology for having to write of women and knights who do wrong. He justifies it, however, by pointing out that even in Heaven, angels sinned (rebelled against God). So is it any wonder if a fallen human sins?

3

Then listen lordings, if ye list° to weet *wish*
The cause, why Satyrane and Paridell
Might not be entertained, as seemed meet,° *appropriate, customary*
Into that castle (as that squire does tell.)[2]
Therein a cankered crabbed churl[3] does dwell,
That has no skill of court nor courtesy,
Nor cares, what men say of him ill or well;
For all his days he drowns in privacy,[4]
Yet has full large° to live, and spend at liberty. *largesse, wealth*

4

But all his mind is set on mucky pelfe,° *filthy money*
To hoard up heaps of evil gotten mass,
For which he others wrongs, and wrecks himself;
Yet is he linked to a lovely lass,
Whose beauty doth her bounty far surpass,[5]
The which to him both far unequal years,
And also far unlike conditions has;
For she does joy to play amongst her peers,
And to be free from hard restraint and jealous fears.

5

But he is old, and withered like hay,
Unfit fair lady's service to supply;
The private guilt whereof makes him always
Suspect her truth, and keep continual spy
Upon her with his other blinked[6] eye;
Nor suffers he resort° of living wight *access*
Approach to her, nor keep her company,
But in close bower her mews° from all men's sight, *keeps confined*
Deprived of kindly joy and natural delight.

---

2. The next few verses consist of the Squire of Dames telling the knights about the occupants of the castle.
3. A very unpleasant fellow.
4. This also indicates secretiveness.
5. She was pretty, but poor.
6. Unclear; perhaps one eye was blinded.

6

Malbecco he, and Hellenore she hight,
Unfitly yoked together in one team,
That is the cause, why never any knight
Is suffered here to enter, but he seem
Such, as no doubt of him he need misdeem.°   *suspect*
Thereat Sir Satyrane began smile, and say,
"Extremely mad the man I surely deem,
That weens° with watch and hard restraint to stay°   *believes / restrain*
A woman's will, which is disposed to go astray.⁷

7

"In vain he fears that, which he cannot shun:
For who wotes° not, that woman's subtleties   *knows*
Can beguile Argus,⁸ when she list misdone?°   *wishes to mistreat*
It is not iron bands, nor hundred eyes,
Nor brazen° walls, nor many wakeful spies,   *brass*
That can withhold her willful wandering feet;
But fast good will with gentle courtesies,
And timely service to her pleasures meet
May her perhaps contain, that else would always flee."

8

"Then is he not more mad," said Paridell,
That hath himself unto such service sold,
In doleful thralldom all his days to dwell?
For sure a fool I do him firmly hold,
That loves his fetters, though they were of gold.
But why do we devise° of others' ill,   *discuss*
Whiles thus we suffer this same dotard° old,   *senile older person*
To keep us out, in scorn of his own will,
And rather do not ransack all, and himself kill?"

9

"Nay let us first," said Satyrane, "entreat
The man by gentle means, to let us in,

---

7. In other words, it is madness to attempt to force a woman's love, especially through holding her prisoner.
8. The giant with one hundred eyes, tricked by the beautiful Io (who had, unfortunately, been turned into a cow by Zeus so his wife wouldn't see her) so that she could escape.

And afterwards affray° with cruel threat, *affright*
Ere that we to enforce it do begin:
Then if all fail, we will by force it win,
And also reward the wretch for his mesprise,° *ill deeds*
As may be worthy of his heinous sin."
That counsel pleased: then Paridell did rise,
And to the castle gate approached in quiet ways.

10

Whereat soft knocking, entrance he desired.
The good man self,° which then the porter played,[9] *himself*
Him answered, that all were now retired
Unto their rest, and all the keys conveyed° *were given*
Unto their master, who in bed was laid,
That none him dared awake out of his dream;
And therefore them of patience gently prayed.° *begged their patience*
Then Paridell began to change his theme,
And threatened him with force and punishment extreme.

11

But all in vain; for naught might him relent,
And now so long before the wicket fast
They waited, that the night was forward spent,[10]
And the fair welkin° foully overcast, *sky*
Began blowing up a bitter stormy blast,
With shower and hail so horrible and dread,
That this fair many° were compelled at last, *company*
To fly for succor to a little shed,
The which beside the gate for swine was ordered.[11]

12

It fortuned, soon after they were gone,
Another knight, whom tempest thither brought,
Came to that castle, and with earnest moan,
Like as the rest, late entrance dearly sought;
But like so as the rest he prayed for naught,

---

9. This is *not* the porter (the gatekeeper). It is Malbecco himself, playing the part.
10. Night had fallen, and the weather was turning foul.
11. They took shelter in a pig shed.

For flatly he of entrance was refused,
Sorely° thereat he was displeased, and thought   *greatly*
How to avenge himself so sore abused,
And evermore the churl of courtesy accused.[12]

13

But to avoid the intolerable storm,
He was compelled to seek some refuge near,
And to that shed, to shroud him from the shower,
He came, which full of guests he found whyleare,[13]
So as he was not let to enter there:
Whereat he began to wax exceeding wrathful,
And swore, that he would lodge with them yfere,°   *together*
Or them dislodge, all were they liefe or loath;[14]
And so defied them each, and so defied them both.[15]

14

Both were full loath to leave that needful tent,
And both full loath in darkness to debate;°   *do battle with*
Yet both full lief° him lodging to have lent,[16]   *willing*
And both full lief his boasting to abate;°   *end*
But chiefly Paridell his heart did grate,
To hear him threaten so despitefully.
As if he did a dog to kennel rated,
That durst not bark; and rather had he die,
Than when he was defied, in coward corner lie.[17]

15

Though hastily remounting to his steed,
He forth issued; like as a boisterous wind,
Which in the earth's hollow caves hath long been hid,
And shut up fast within her prisons blind,

---

12. In other words, accused him of violating the rules of courtesy.
13. The pigpen was filled with our other heroes before the new knight arrived.
14. Whether they liked it or not.
15. Both of the knights. No honorable knight would fight a squire.
16. Unclear. Perhaps they felt that if the knight had asked in a nicer manner, they might have lent him some room.
17. In other words, he would rather die than stay in a corner when challenged.

Makes the huge element[18] against her kind°   *nature*
To move, and tremble as it were aghast,
Until that it an issue forth may find;
Then forth it breaks, and with his furious blast
Confounds both land and seas, and skies doth overcast.

16

Their steel-head spears they strongly couched,[19] and met
Together with impetuous rage and force,
That with the terror of their fierce attack,
They rudely drove to ground both man and horse,
That each awhile lay like a senseless corpse.
But Paridell sore bruised with the blow,
Could not arise, the counterchange to scorse,[20]
Until that young squire him reared from below;
Then drew he his bright sword, and began about him throw.

17

But Satyrane forth stepping, did them stay
And with fair entreaty pacified their ire,
Then when they were accorded from the fray,°   *fight*
Against that castle's lord they began conspire,
To heap on him due vengeance for his hire.°   *that he earned*
They been agreed, and to the gates they go
To burn the same with unquenchable fire,
And that uncourteous churl, their common foe,
To do foul death to die, or wrap in grievous woe.

18

Malbecco seeing them resolved indeed
To flame the gates, and hearing them to call
For fire in earnest, ran with fearful speed,
And to them calling from the castle wall,
Besought them humbly, him to bear withal,
As ignorant of servant's bad abuse,[21]

---

18. The earth.
19. They put their spears in the position for attack.
20. In other words, he couldn't arise to "counterchange" (give and receive) another set of blows.
21. Malbecco claims it was a servant, not he, who denied them entrance.

And slack attendance unto strangers call.
The knights were willing all things to excuse,
Though naught believed, entrance late did not refuse.²²

19

They been brought into a comely bower,
And served of all things that might needful be;
Yet secretly their host did on them glower,
And welcomed more for fear, than charity;
But they dissembled,° what they did not see,   *faked it*
And welcomed themselves. Each began undight°   *undress*
Their garments wet, and weary armor free,
To dry themselves by Vulcan's flaming light,°   *by the fire*
And also their lately bruised parts to bring in plight.°   *to treat*

20

And also that stranger knight amongst the rest;
Was for like need forced to disarray:°   *remove armor*
Though when veiled was her lofty crest,
Her golden locks, that were in tramells° gay   *braids*
Upbound, did themselves down display,
And reached unto her heels; like sunny beams,
That in a cloud their light did long time stay,
Their vapor vaded,²³ show their golden gleams,
And through the piercing air shoot forth their azure streams.²⁴

21

She also doffed her heavy habergeon,°   *chain mail*
Which the fair feature of her limbs did hide,
And her well plighted frock, which she did wont°   *did usually*
To tuck about her short, when she did ride,
She low let fall, that flowed from her lank side
Down to her foot, with careless modesty.
Then of them all she plainly was espied,
To be a woman wight, unwist° to be,   *unknown*
The fairest woman wight that ever eye did see.

22. They didn't believe or trust him, but they entered into the castle.
23. As if the clouds had cleared away.
24. A little unclear. "Azure" is blue; perhaps he is referring to the sky, when the sun's beams pierce through it.

22

Like as Minerva, being late returned
From slaughter of the giants conquered;
Where proud Encelade,[25] whose wide nostrils burned
With breathed flames, like to a furnace red,
Transfixed with the spear, down tumbled dead
From top of Hemus,° by him heaped high; *a Greek mountain*
Hath loosed her helmet from her lofty head,
And her Gorgonian shield[26] begins to untie
From her left arm, to rest in glorious victory.

23

Which when they beheld, they smitten were
With great amazement of so wondrous sight,
And each on other, and they all on her
Stood gazing, as if sudden great affright
Had them surprised. At last avizing° right, *realizing*
Her goodly personage and glorious hue,
Which they so much mistook, they took delight
In their first error, and yet still anew
With wonder of her beauty fed their hungry view.

24

Yet not their hungry view be satisfied,
But seeing still the more desired to see,
And ever firmly fixed did abide
In contemplation of divinity:
But most they marveled at her chivalry,
And noble prowess, which they had approved,° *tested*
That much they fained° to know, who she might be; *wished*
Yet none of all them her thereof moved,
Yet every one her liked, and every one her loved.

25

And Paridell though partly discontent
With his late fall, and foul indignity,[27]

---

25. One of Minerva's enemies.
26. Minerva's shield bore the image of the Gorgon.
27. Remember, he was knocked down by a woman.

Yet was soon won° his malice to relent,   *won over*
Through gracious regard of her fair eye,
And knightly worth, which he too late did try,
Yet tried did adore. Supper was dight;°   *prepared*
Then they Malbecco prayed of courtesy,
That of his lady they might have the sight,
And company at meal, to do them more delight.

26

But he to shift their curious request,
Began cause, why she could not come in place;
Her crased° health, her late recourse to rest,   *ill*
And humid evening ill for sick folk's case:
But none of those excuses could take place;[28]
Nor would they eat, until she in presence came.
She° came in presence with right comely grace,   *Hellenore*
And fairly them saluted, as became,
And showed herself in all a gentle courteous dame.

27

They sat to meat, and Satyrane his chance
Was her before, and Paridell beside;
But he himself° sat looking subtle askance,   *Malbecco*
Against Britomart, and ever closely eyed
Sir Satyrane, that glances might not glide:
But his blind eye, that sided Paridell,
All his demeanor from his sight did hide:
On her fair face so did he feed his fill,
And sent close messages of love to her at will.[29]

28

And ever and anon, when none was aware,
With speaking looks, that close embassies° bore,   *messages*
He roved° at her, and told his secret care: *shot (as an arrow) looks at her*
For all that art he learned had of yore.
Nor was she ignorant of that lewd lore,

---

28. None were found acceptable.
29. Paridell, out of sight of Malbecco, flirts with Hellenore.

But in his eye his meaning wisely read,
And with the like him answered evermore:
She sent at him one fiery dart, whose head
Poisoned was with privy lust, and jealous dread.[30]

29

He° from that deadly throw made no defense,   *Paridell*
But to the wound his weak heart opened wide;
The wicked engine through false influence,
Past through his eyes, and secretly did glide
Into his heart, which it did sorely gryde.°   *pierce*
But nothing new to him° was that same pain,   *Paridell*
Nor pain at all; for he so oft had tried
The power thereof, and loved so oft in vain,
That thing of course he counted, love to entertain.

30

Thenceforth to her he sought to intimate
His inward grief, by means to him well known,
Now Bacchus fruit out of the silver plate
He on the table dashed, as overthrown,[31]
Or of the fruitful liquor overflowed,
And by the dancing bubbles did divine,
Or therein write to let his love be shown;
Which well she read out of the learned line,[32]
A sacrament profane in mystery of wine.

31

And when so of his hand the pledge she raught,°   *took*
The guilty cup she feigned to mistake,
And in her lap did shed her idle draught,[33]
Showing desire her inward flame to slake:°   *satisfy*
By such close signs they secret way did make
Unto their wills, and one eye's watch escape;[34]

30. Hellenore is flirting with Paridell. This is what Malbecco dreads.
31. This is a code; Paridell spills his wine as a sign to Hellenore of his lust for her.
32. He could be writing something with the spilled wine; she recognizes the game and reciprocates.
33. She spilled the wine into her own lap. The significance is obvious.
34. They avoided Malbecco's one eye's gaze.

CANTO IX.

Two eyes him needed, for to watch and wake,
Who lovers will deceive. Thus was the ape,
By their fair handling, put into Malbecco's cape.³⁵

32

Now when of meats and drinks they had their fill,
Purpose was moved³⁶ by that gentle dame,
Unto those knights adventurous, to tell
Of deeds of arms, which unto them became,
And everyone his kindred, and his name.
Then Paridell, in whom a kindly pride
Of gracious speech, and skill his words to frame
Abounded, being glad of so fit time
Him to commend to her,³⁷ thus spoke, of all well eyed.

33

"Troy, that art now naught but an idle name,
And in thine ashes buried low dost lie,
Though whilome° far much greater then thy fame,   *in former times*
Before that angry gods, and cruel sky³⁸
Upon thee heaped a direful destiny,
What boots it boast thy glorious descent,³⁹
And fetch from heaven thy great genealogy,
Since all thy worthy praises being blent,°   *stained*
Their offspring hath embased, and later glory shent.⁴⁰

34

"Most famous worthy of the world, by whom
That war was kindled, which did Troy inflame,
And stately towers of Ilion° whilome   *another name for Troy*
Brought unto baleful ruin, was by name
Sir Paris far renowned through noble fame,

---

35. This is a metaphor for tricking Malbecco. The ape symbolizes foolishness, and, when they "put" him into Malbecco's "cape," they made a fool of him.
36. It was proposed that they speak of their adventures.
37. This was his chance to further impress Hellenore.
38. Remember, the gods and goddesses took sides in the Trojan War.
39. "What use (boots) is it to boast of Trojan ancestry?"
40. *Embased* means "to be brought low"; *shent* means "shamed."

Who through great prowess and bold hardiness,
From Lacedæmon° fetched the fairest dame, *Sparta*
That ever Greece did boast, or knight possess,
Whom Venus to him gave for meed° of worthiness.⁴¹ *reward*

35

"Fair Helen, flower of beauty excellent,
And garland of the mighty conquerors,
That made many ladies dear lament
The heavy loss of their brave paramours,⁴²
Which they far off beheld from Trojan towers,
And saw the fields of fair Scamander° strewn *a Trojan river*
With carcasses of noble warriors,
Whose fruitless lives were under furrow sown,
And Xanthus° sandy banks with blood all overflowing. *the same river*

36

"From him° my linage I derive aright, *Paris*
Who long before the ten years' siege of Troy,
Whiles yet on Ida° he a shepherd hight, *Mount Ida*
On fair Oenone° begot a lovely boy, *a faerie nymph*
Whom for remembrance of her passed joy,
She of his father Paris did name;
Who, after Greeks did Priam's° realm destroy, *King of Troy*
Gathered the Trojan relics saved from flame,
And with them sailing thence, to the isle of Paros came.

37

"That was by him called Paros,° which before *a Greek island*
Hight Nausa, there he many years did reign,
And built Nausicle° by the Pontic⁴³ shore, *a new city*
The which he dying left next in remain° *in line*
To Paridas his son.
From whom I Paridell by kin descend;
But for fair ladies' love, and glory's gain,

---

41. Come on, you know the story. The beauty contest, the golden apple, Helen of Troy?
42. Many women mourned the loss of their lovers in the war.
43. The Greek word for "sea."

My native soil have left, my days to spend
In pursuing deeds of arms, my lives and labors end."

38

When the noble Britomart heard tell
Of Trojan wars, and Priam's city sacked,
The rueful story of Sir Paridell,
She was impassioned at that piteous act,
With zealous envy of Greeks' cruel act,
Against that nation, from whose race of old
She heard, that she was lineally extract:°   *descended*
For noble Britons sprung from Trojans bold,
And Troynovant° was built of old Troy's ashes cold.⁴⁴   *"New Troy"*

39

Then sighing soft awhile, at last she thus:
"O lamentable fall of famous town,
Which reigned so many years victorious,
And of all Asia bore the sovereign crown,
In one sad night consumed, and thrown down:
What stony heart, that hears thy hapless fate,
Is not pierced with deep compassion,
And makes example of man's wretched state,⁴⁵
That flowers so fresh at morn, and fades at evening late?

40

"Behold, Sir, how your pitiful complaint
Hath found another partner of your pain:
For nothing may impress so dear constraint,
As country's cause, and common foes' disdain.⁴⁶
But if it should not grieve you, back again
To turn your course, I would to hear desire,°   *desire to hear*
What to Aeneas fell; since that men say
He was not in the city's woeful fire
Consumed, but did himself to safety retire."

44. According to certain myths, some of the Trojans sailed to Britain and founded its earliest kingdoms. Britomart certainly thinks so.
45. Serves as a cautionary tale.
46. In other words, what can move a person as much as patriotism for his (or her) country?

41

"Anchyses son begot of Venus fair,"[47]
Said he, "out of the flames for safeguard fled,
And with a remnant did to sea repair,°   *flee*
Where he through fated error° long was led   *wanderings*
Full many years, and weetless° wandered   *unknowingly*
From shore to shore, amongst the Lybian sands,
Ere rest he found. Much there he suffered,
And many perils past in foreign lands,
To save his people sad from victors' vengeful hands.

42

"At last in Latium° he did arrive,   *Italy*
Where he with cruel war was entertained
Of the inland folk, which sought him back to drive,
Until he with old Latinus was constrained,
To contract wedlock (so the fates ordained).[48]
Wedlock contract in blood, and also in blood
Accomplished, that many dear° complained: *earnestly*
The rival slain, the victor through the flood[49]
Escaped hardly, hardly praised his wedlock good.

43

"Yet after all, he victor did survive,
And with Latinus did the kingdom part.
But after when both nations began to strive,
Into their names the title to convert,[50]
His son Julus did from thence depart,
With all the warlike youth of Trojans' blood,
And in long Alba° placed his throne apart,   *a region of Latium*
Where fair it flourished, and long time it stood,
Until Romulus renewing it, to Rome removed."

---

47. Aeneas' father, Anchyses, was a mortal. Venus was decidedly not.
48. In other words, peace came only through Aeneas' marriage to the daughter of Latinus, the king of Latium.
49. Turnus, king of the Rutuli wanted to marry Latinus' daughter; he went to battle with the Trojans to win her, and much blood flowed (that's the "flood" part) before Aeneas killed him.
50. In other words, to add their names to their countries.

44

"There there," said Britomart, "fresh appeared
The glory of the later world to spring,
And Troy again out of her dust was reared,°   *raised*
To sit in second seat of sovereign king,
Of all the world under her governing.
But a third kingdom yet is to arise,[51]
Out of the Trojans' scattered offspring,
That in all glory and great enterprise,
Both first and second Troy shall dare to equalize.

45

"It Troynovant is hight, that with the waves
Of wealthy Thames washed is along,[52]
Upon whose stubborn neck, whereat he raves
With roaring rage, and sore° himself does throng,°   *greatly / crowd*
That all men fear to tempt his billows strong,
She[53] fastened hath her foot, which stands so high,
That it a wonder of the world is sung
In foreign lands, and all which pass by,
Beholding it from far, do think it threatens the sky.

46

"The Trojan Brutus did first that city found,
And Highgate made the mere thereof by west,[54]
And Overgate by north: that is the bound
Toward the land; two rivers bound the rest.
So huge a scope at first him seemed best,
To be the compass of his kingdom's seat:
So huge a mind could not in lesser rest,
Nor in small meres° contain his glory great,   *boundaries*
That Albion° had conquered first by warlike feat."   *another name for Britain*

---

51. Here, Britomart is prophesying that a third Troy will arise—Britain.
52. Yes, the river in London. "Troynovant" ("New Troy," you'll recall) was a reference to London.
53. Believe it or not, we're now talking about the London Bridge ("She").
54. Highgate is an area in northern London; *mere* means "boundaries." Brutus is laying out his new city.

47

"Ah fairest lady knight," said Paridell
"Pardon I pray my heedless oversight,
Who had forgot, that whilome° I heard tell　　　　　　　　　*formerly*
From aged Mnemon;[55] for my wits been light.[56]
Indeed," he said, "(if I remember right)
That of the antique Trojan stock, there grew
Another plant, that reached to wondrous height,
And far abroad his mighty branches threw,
Into the utmost angle° of the world he knew.　　　　　　　　　*corner*

48

"For that same Brutus, whom much he did advance
In all his speech, was Sylvius his son[57]
Whom having slain, through luckless arrow's glance
He fled for fear of that he had done,
Or else for shame, so foul reproach to shun,
And with him led to sea a youthful train,°　　　　　　　　　*young followers*
Where weary wandering they long time did wonne,[58]
And many fortunes proved in the ocean main,
And great adventures found, that now were long to say.

49

"At last by fatal course they driven were
Into an island° spacious and broad,　　　　　　　　　*the British isles*
The furthest North, that did to them appear:
Which after rest they seeking far abroad,
Found it the fittest soil for their abode,
Fruitful of all things fit for living food,
But wholly waste,° and void of people's tread,　　　　　　　　　*wasteland*
Save an huge nation of the giants' brood,
That fed on living flesh, and drank men's vital blood.

---

55. Unclear. The word is Greek for "mindful." Perhaps he is saying he's reminded of something.
56. My mind was getting forgetful.
57. Brutus was the son of Sylvius. As a child, he accidently killed his father, then fled from shame.
58. In this case, *wonne* means "live."

50

"Whom he through weary wars and labors long,
Subdued with loss of many Britons bold:
In which the great Goemagot of strong
Corineus, and Coulin of Debon old[59]
Were overthrown and laid on the earth full cold,
Which quaked under their so hideous mass,
A famous history to be enrolled
In everlasting monuments of brass,
That all the antique worthies' merits far did pass.

51

"His° work great Troynovant, his work is eke   *Brutus*
Fair Lincoln, both renowned far away,
That who from east to west will endlong seek,
Cannot two fair cities find this day,
Except Cleopolis:° so heard I say   *the Faerie Queene's city*
Old Mnemon. Therefore sir,[60] I greet you well
Your country kin, and you entirely pray
Of pardon for the strife, which late befell
Betwixt us both unknown." So ended Paridell.

52

But all the while, that he these speeches spent,
Upon his lips hung fair dame Hellenore,[61]
With vigilant regard, and due attention,
Fashioning worlds of fancies evermore
In her frail wit, that now her quite forlorn:
The whiles unawares away her wandering eye,
And greedy ears her weak heart from her bore:
Which he perceiving, ever privately
In speaking, many false belgardes° at her let fly.   *looks of love (or lust)*

---

59. These were some of the giants.
60. Paridell is talking to Britomart; he refers to her as "sir," perhaps, as a courtesy due to another knight. In this passage, he is apologizing for attacking a fellow countrywoman.
61. In other words, he was speaking to impress her.

53

So long these knights discoursed diversely,
Of strange affairs, and noble hardiness,
Which they had passed with much jeopardy,
That now the humid night was far forth spent,
And heavenly lamps were halfway ybrent:° *burned*
Which the old man seeing well, who too long thought
Every discourse and every argument,
Which by the hours he measured, besought
Them go to rest. So all unto their bowers were brought.

Match the Spenserian words to their modern meanings.

redoubted	*suspects*
read	*respected*
pelfe	*revealed*
misdeeme	*sky*
wotes	*money*
devise	*together*
mesprise	*knows*
welkin	*ill deeds*
yfere	*end*
abate	*discuss*

1. Why does Malbecco deny the knights entrance to his castle?

2. The knights are forced to shelter in a pig shed. What might this symbolize? Remember, nothing happens in *The Faerie Queene* without a meaning attached—usually several.

3. How does Sir Paridell prove to be a disappointment in this Canto? Why?

Canto X.

Paridell rapeth[1] Hellenore:
Malbecco her pursues:
Finds amongst Satyrs, whence with him
To return she doth refuse.

1

The morrow next, so soon as Phoebus Lamp
Bewrayed[2] had the world with early light,
And fresh Aurora° had the shady damp   *the dawn*
Out of the goodly heaven moved quite,
Fair Britomart and that same Faerie knight°   *Satyrane*
Uprose, forth on their journey for to wend:
But Paridell complained, that his late fight[3]
With Britomart, so sore did him offend,°   *wound*
That ride he could not, till his hurts he did amend.°   *heal*

2

So forth they fared, but he behind them stayed,
Maulgre[4] his host, who grudged° grievously,   *begrudgingly agreed*
To house a guest, that would be needs obeyed,°   *that needs to be obeyed*
And of his own him left not liberty:
Might wanting measure moves surquedry.[5]
Two things he feared, but the third was death;
That fierce young man's unruly mastery;

---

1. As you'll see, this means "abduct," not "ravage."
2. Throughout this book, I have usually translated *bewrayed* in the text to "betrayed." Here, however, it means more "to reveal" (though the meanings are close, I admit), so I'm leaving it alone.
3. He's talking of when Britomart beat him up. I love this girl.
4. To the great consternation of his host.
5. Complicated, but basically, Malbecco didn't leave Paridell alone (at "liberty"), because if Paridell was treated too grandly, that might lead to "surquedry," or arrogance. In truth, Malbecco feared Paridell would be so presumptuous that he would take his wife.

His money, which he loved as living breath;
And his fair wife, whom honest long he kept uneasily.[6]

3

But patience perforce; he must abide,
What fortune and his fate on him will lay,
Fond° is the fear, that finds no remedy;   *foolish*
Yet warily he watches every way,
By which he feared evil happen may:
So the evil thinks by watching to prevent;
Nor doth he suffer her, nor night, nor day,
Out of his sight herself once to absent.
So doth he punish her and also himself torment.

4

But Paridell kept better watch, then he,
A fit occasion for his turn to find:[7]
False love, why do men say, thou cannot see,
And in their foolish fancy feign thee blind,
That with thy charms[8] the sharpest sight doest bind,
And to thy will abuse? Thou walks free,
And sees every secret of the mind;
Thou sees all, yet none at all sees thee;
All that is by the working of thy divinity.°   *Cupid*

5

So perfect in that art was Paridell,
That he Malbecco's halfen eye[9] did wile,°   *trick*
His halfen eye he wiled wondrous well,
And Hellenore both eyes did also beguile,
Both eyes and heart at once, during the while
That he there sojourned his wounds to heal;

---

6. Notice which Spenser mentions first—Malbecco was a coward. He also loved his money, and even his wife (in a strange way). This brings to mind Shakespeare's *The Merchant of Venice,* when Shylock (learning his daughter had fled) cried, "My daughter, my ducats!"—worried, it seems, as much about the money.
7. Paridell watched and waited for his opportunity with Hellenore. And he was better at it than Malbecco.
8. Here, Spenser is speaking of Paridell's attempts to charm (really, to seduce) Hellenore. Spenser goes on to say it seemed he was aided by Cupid.
9. Remember, Malbecco was blind in one eye and half-blind in the other.

That Cupid himself it seeing, close did smile,
To weet how he her love away did steal,
And bade, that none their joyous treason should reveal.

6

The learned lover lost no time nor tide,[10]
That least advantage might to him afford,
Yet bore so fair a sail,[11] that none espied
His secret drift, till he her laid aboard.
When so in open place, and common board,°   *table*
He fortuned her to meet, with common speech
He courted her, yet baited every word,
That his ungentle host did not him impeach°   *accuse*
Of vile ungentleness, or hospitality breach.

7

But when apart (if ever her apart)
He found, then his false engines fast he plied,[12]
And all the sleights embosomed in his heart;[13]
He sighed, he sobbed, he swooned, he perdy died,[14]
And cast himself on ground her fast beside:
Though when again he him bethought to live,
He wept, and wailed, and false laments belied,
Saying, but if she mercy would him give
That he might anyway die, yet did his death forgive.

8

And other whiles with amorous delights,
And pleasing toys he would her entertain,
Now singing sweetly, to surprise her spirits,
Now making lays° of love and lover's pain,   *songs*
Bransles, ballads, virelays,[15] and verses vain;

---

10. He got right down to business.
11. The texts differ, but Spenser is making a nautical metaphor. He's saying Paridell pursued Hellenore as a pirate ship might pursue its prey.
12. His "false engines" are his dishonorable designs on her.
13. All the tricks he knew by heart.
14. He swore he would, by God, die without her.
15. These are various kinds of songs; bransles are dancing songs, you know about ballads, and virelays were a French sort of song.

Oft purposes, oft riddles he devised,
And thousands like, which flowed in his brain,
With which he fed her fancy, and enticed
To take to his new love, and leave her old despised.

9

And everywhere he might, and every while
He did her service dutiful, and served
At hand with humble pride, and pleasing guile,
So closely yet, that none but she it viewed,
Who well perceived all, and all indewed.°   *took in*
Thus finely did he his false nets spread,
With which he many weak hearts had subdued
Of yore, and many had like misled:
What wonder then, if she were likewise carried?

10

No fort so defensible, no walls so strong,
But that continual battery will rive,°   *break*
Or daily siege through dispurvayance° long,   *lack of food and water*
And lack of rescues will to parley drive;°   *seek terms*
And Peace, that unto parley ear will give,
Will shortly yield itself, and will be made
The vassal of the victors will bylive:°   *in a lively or speedy manner*
That stratagem had oftentimes assayed°   *attempted*
This crafty paramour, and now it plain displayed.

11

For through his trains he her entrapped hath,
That she her love and heart hath wholly sold
To him, without regard of gain, or scath,°   *penalty, harm*
Or care of credit, or of husband old,
Whom she hath vowed to dub a fair cuckold.[16]
Naught wants but time and place, which shortly she
Devised hath, and to her lover told.
It pleased well. So well they both agree;
So ready ripe to ill, ill women's counsels be.[17]

---

16. A cuckold is a man whose wife is unfaithful.
17. So ready to sin; the second part ("ill women's counsels be") indicates the plans she made to leave with another man (Paridell).

12

Dark was the evening, fit for lovers' stealth,
When chanced Malbecco busy be elsewhere,
She to his closet went, where all his wealth
Lay hid: thereof she countless sums did rear,°   *raise*
The which she meant away with her to bear;
The rest she fired° for sport, or for despite;°   *set on fire / spite*
As Hellen, when she saw aloft appear
The Trojan flames, and reach to heaven's height
Did clap her hands, and joyed at that doleful sight.

13

This second Helen, fair dame Hellenore,
The while her husband ran with sorrowful haste,
To quench the flames, which she had tyned° before,   *started*
Laughed at his foolish labor spent in waste;
And ran into her lover's arms right fast;
Where straight embraced, she to him° did cry,   *Malbecco*
And call aloud for help, ere help were past;
For lo, that guest would bear her forcibly,[18]
And meant to ravish her, that rather had to die.[19]

14

The wretched man° hearing her call for aid,   *Malbecco*
And ready seeing him with her to flee,
In his disquiet mind was much dismayed:
But when again he backward cast his eye,
And saw the wicked fire so furiously
Consume his heart,° and scorch his idol's face,   *his heart's true desire*
He was therewith distressed diversely,
Nor wist° he how to turn, nor to what place;   *knew*
Was never wretched man in such a woeful case.

15

Ay when to him she cried, to her he turned,
And left the fire; love money overcame:

---

18. She's crying "wolf" here. She's the one who came up with the plan, remember?
19. She claims she would rather die than be raped.

But when he marked, how his money burned,
He left his wife; money did love disclaim:
Both was he loath to lose his loved dame,
And loath to leave his liefest pelfe° behind,   *beloved money*
Yet since he could not save both, he saved that same,
Which was the dearest to his dunghill mind,
The food of his desire, the joy of misers blind.

16

Thus while all things in troublous uproar were,
And all men busy to suppress the flame,
The loving couple[20] need no rescue fear,
But leisure had, and liberty to frame°   *accomplish*
Their purposed flight, free from all men's reclaim;
And night, the patroness of love-stealth fair,
Gave them safe conduct, until to end they came:
So been they gone together, a wanton pair
Of lovers loosely knit, where list them to repair.

17

Soon as the cruel flames slaked were,
Malbecco seeing, how his loss did lie,
Out of the flames, which he had quench whylere°   *before*
Into huge waves of grief and jealousy
Full deeply plunged was, and drowned nye,°   *nearly drowned*
Twixt inward dole° and felonious° spite;   *sorrow / malignant*
He raved, he wept, he stamped, he loud did cry,
And all the passions, that in man may light,
Did him at once oppress, and vex his captive spirit.

18

Long thus he chewed the cud of inward grief,
And did consume his gall with anguish sore,
Still when he mused on his late mischance,
Then still the smart° thereof increased more,   *pain*
And seemed more grievous, then it was before:
At last when sorrow he saw booted naught,°   *proved useless*

---

20. Spenser is being ironic here; this wasn't real love. This was lust gone bad.

Nor grief might not his love to him restore,
He began devise how her he rescue might;
Ten thousand ways he cast° in his confused thought.   *planned*

19

At last resolving, like a pilgrim poor,
To search her forth, where so she might be found,
And bearing with him treasure in close store,
The rest he leaves in ground: so takes in hand°   *takes it upon himself*
To seek her endlessly, both by sea and land.
Long he her sought, he sought her far and near,
And everywhere that he might understand,
Of knights and ladies any meetings were,
And of each one he met, he tidings did inquire.

20

But all in vain, his woman was too wise,
Ever to come into his clutch again,
And he too simple ever to surprise
The jolly[21] Paridell, for all his pain.
One day, as he passed by the plain
With weary pace, he far away espied
A couple, seeming well to be his twain,[22]
Which hovered close under a forest side,
As if they lay in wait, or else themselves did hide.

21

Well weened he that those the same might be,
And as he better did their shape advise,°   *see*
Him seemed more their manner did agree;
For the one was armed all in warlike ways,
Whom, to be Paridell he did devise;°   *assume*
And the other all clad in garments light,
Colored like to womanish disguise,
He did resemble to his lady bright;
And ever his faint heart much yearned at the sight.

---

21. In this sense, *jolly* means "prideful."
22. "His twain" as in "the two he searches for."

Amazons

Who were the Amazons? They formed a mythical nation of women only. They were said to have lived in Pontus (part of what is now Turkey).

No men were permitted to live in their country. To prevent the dying out of their race, once a year they paid a visit to a neighboring tribe. Only the female children resulting from this visit were kept. The boys were either killed or sent back to their fathers in the neighboring tribe.

The girls were brought up to be fierce warriors. In one myth, they are said to have been assisted in battle by a young Priam, king of Troy. That's why they assist him in the Trojan War, in his later years.

The Greek historian Herodotus wrote of them. Here's what he had to say in a 1920 translation by A. D. Godly:

> About the Sauromatae, the story is as follows. When the Greeks were at war with the Amazons (whom the Scythians call Oiorpata, a name signifying in our tongue killers of men, for in Scythian a man is "oior" and to kill is "pata"), the story runs that after their victory on the Thermodon they sailed away carrying in three ships as many Amazons as they had been able to take alive; and out at sea the Amazons attacked the crews and killed them.
>
> But they knew nothing about ships, or how to use rudder or sail or oar; and with the men dead, they were at the mercy of waves and winds, until they came to the Cliffs by the Maeetian lake; this place is in the country of the free Scythians. The Amazons landed there, and set out on their journey to the inhabited country, and seizing the first troop of horses they met, they mounted them and raided the Scythian lands.
>
> The Scythians could not understand the business; for they did not recognize the women's speech or their dress or their nation, but wondered where they had come from, and imagined them to be men all of the same age; and they met the Amazons in battle. The result of the fight was that the Scythians got possession of the dead, and so came to learn that their foes were women. (*Histories* 4.110-111)

22

And ever fain he towards them would go,
But yet dared not for dread approaching near,
But stood aloof, unweeting what to do;
Until that pricked forth with love's extremity,
That is the father of foul jealousy,
He closely nearer crept, the truth to weet:
But, as he nearer drew, he easily
Might discern, that it was not his sweetest sweet,
Nor yet her Belamour,° the partner of his sheet.   *lover*

23

But it was scornful Braggadocchio,
That with his servant Trompart hovered there,
Since late he fled from his too earnest foe:
Whom such when as Malbecco spied clear,
He turned back, and would have fled arear;
Until Trompart running hastily, him did stay,
And bade before his sovereign lord appear:
That was him loath, yet dared he not gainsay,°   *refuse*
And coming him before, low louted on the lay.[23]

24

The boaster at him sternly bent his brow,
As if he could have killed him with his look,
That to the ground him meekly made to bow,
And awful terror deep into him struck,
That every member of his body quaked.
Said he,° "Thou man of naught, what does thou here,   *Braggadocchio*
Unfitly furnished with thy bag and book,
Where I expected one with shield and spear,
To prove some deeds of arms upon an equal peer."

25

The wretched man at his imperious speech,
Was all abashed, and low prostrating, said,
"Good Sir, let not my rudeness° be no breach   *roughness*

---

23. He bowed low to the ground. He doesn't know Braggadocchio like we do.

Unto your patience, nor be ill paid;°   *ill-served, abused*
For I unawares this way by fortune strayed,
A silly pilgrim driven to distress,
That seek a lady." There he sudden stayed,
And did the rest with grievous sighs suppress,
While tears stood in his eyes, few drops of bitterness.

26

"What lady, man?" said Trompart, "take good heart,
And tell thy grief, if any hidden lay;
Was never better time to show thy smart°   *problems*
Than now, that noble succor° is thee by,   *powerful aid*
That is the whole world's common remedy."
That cheerful word his weak heart much did cheer,°   *lift up*
And with vain hope his spirits faint supply,
That bold he said, "O most redoubted° peer,   *respected nobleman*
Vouchsafe with mild regard a wretch's case to hear."

27

Then sighing sore,° "It is not long," said he,°   *greatly / Malbecco*
"Since I enjoyed the gentlest dame alive;
Of whom a knight, no knight at all perdy,°   *as God knows*
But shame of all, that do for honor strive,
By treacherous deceit did me deprive;
Through open outrage he her bore away,
And with foul force unto his will did drive,
Which all good knights, that arms do bear this day,
Are bound for to revenge, and punish if they may.

28

"And you most noble lord, that can and dare
Redress° the wrong of miserable wight,   *repair*
Cannot employ your most victorious spear
In better quarrel, than defense of right,
And for a lady against a faithless knight,
So shall your glory be advanced much,
And all fair ladies magnify your might,
And also myself, although I simple such,
Your worthy pain shall well reward with guerdon° rich."   *reward for your efforts*

29

With that out of his bag forth he drew
Great store of treasure, therewith him to tempt;
But he on it looked scornfully askew,[24]
As much disdaining to be so misdeemed,°   *misunderstood*
Or a war-monger to be basely named,
And said, "Thy offers base I greatly loath,
And also thy words uncourteous and unkempt;°   *rough*
I tread in dust thee and thy money both,
That, were it not for shame . . ."[25] So turned from him wroth.°   *angrily*

30

But Trompart, that his master's humor° knew,   *nature*
In lofty looks to hide an humble mind,
Was inwardly tickled with that golden view,[26]
And in his ear him rounded[27] close behind:
Yet stooped he not, but lay still in the wind,
Waiting advantage on the prey to seize;
Until Trompart lowly to the ground inclined,
Besought him his great courage to appease,
And pardon simple man, that rash did him displease.

31

Big looking like a doughty doucepere,[28]
At last he° thus: "Thou clod of vilest clay,   *Braggadocchio says*
I pardon yield, and with thy rudeness bear;
But weet° henceforth that all that golden prey,°   *know / reward*
And all that else the vain world vaunted may,
I loath as doing, nor deem my due reward:[29]
Fame is my meed,° and glory virtue's pay.   *reward*
But minds of mortal men are muchell° marred,   *much*
And moved amiss with massive muck's unmeet regard.[30]

---

24. Braggadocchio, who doesn't *do* anything, looked scornfully aside from the proffered reward.
25. He cuts off his own sentence, in seeming disgust.
26. He liked the looks of that gold.
27. Trompart whispered to his master.
28. One of the mighty knights of France.
29. He's saying he won't do it for reward (alone) but for glory (and he'll graciously overlook Malbecco's lowly status).
30. "Men are much prone to sin."

32

"And more, I grant to thy great misery
Gracious respect, thy wife shall back be sent,
And that vile knight, whoever that he be,
Which hath thy lady reft,° and knighthood shent,°   *stolen / shamed*
By Sanglamort my sword,[31] whose deadly dent
The blood hath of so many thousands shed,
I swear, ere long shall dearly it repent;
Nor he twixt heaven and earth shall hide his head,
But soon he shall be found, and shortly done be dead."

33

The foolish man thereat was wondrous blithe,°   *happy*
As if the word so spoken, were half done,
And humbly thanked him a thousand since,
That had from death to life him newly won.
Then forth the boaster marching, brave began
His stolen steed[32] to thunder furiously,
As if he heaven and hell would overrun,
And all the world confound with cruelty,
That much Malbecco joyed in his jollity.[33]

34

Thus long they three together travailed,
Through many a wood, and many an uncouth way,
To seek his wife, that was far wandered:
But those two sought naught, but the present prey,[34]
To weet the treasure, which he did bewray,
On which their eyes and hearts were wholly set,
With purpose, how they might it best betray;°   *betray*
For since the hour, that first he did them let
The same behold, therewith their keen desires were whet.°   *stimulated*

---

31. His sword's name (in true Braggadocchio style) is "Bloody Death."
32. In Book II he had stolen Sir Guyon's horse.
33. Again, here *jolly* (or jollity) means pride.
34. In other words, their real interest was in Malbecco's money—not his mission. Their minds were focused on how to get the money from him without having to fight anyone—at least, anyone who might win.

35

It fortuned as they together fared,
They spied, where Paridell came pricking fast
Upon the plain, the which himself prepared
To joust with that brave stranger knight a cast,°   *he planned*
As on adventure by the way he passed:
Alone he rode without his paragon;[35]
For having filched her bells, her up he cast[36]
To the wide world, and let her flee alone,
He wouldn't be clogged.[37] So had he served many one.

36

The gentle lady, loose at random left,
The green-wood long did walk, and wander wide
At wild adventure, like a forlorn waif,
Until on a day the satyrs[38] her espied
Straying alone without groom or guide;
Her up they took, and with them home her led,
With them as housewife ever to abide,
To milk their goats, and make them cheese and bread,
And every one as common good her handled.[39]

37

That shortly she Malbecco has forgot,
And also Sir Paridell, all were he dear;
Who from her went to seek another lot,
And now by fortune was arrived here,
Where those two guilers° with Malbecco were: *tricksters*
Soon as the old man saw Sir Paridell,
He fainted, and was almost dead with fear,
Nor word he had to speak, his grief to tell,

---

35. Without Hellenore.
36. Short version: He had sexual intercourse with her, then threw her away, having taken her virtue.
37. Blocked or slowed from his adventures.
38. Yes, you may think Mr. Tumnus from *The Lion, the Witch and the Wardrobe*. These are good satyrs and kind.
39. They all treated her as their common good—Spenser means "property" but not in a bad or slavery sense. They treated her as a precious possession.

But to him louted low,° and greeted goodly well. — *bowed to*

38

And after asked him for Hellenore,
"I take no keep of her,"[40] said Paridell,
"She wonneth° in the forest there before."[41] — *liveth*
So forth he rode, as his adventure fell;
The whiles the boaster from his lofty sell° — *saddle*
Fained to alight, something amiss to mend;[42]
But the fresh swain° would not his leisure dwell, — *Paridell*
But went his way; whom when he passed kenned,[43]
He up remounted light, and after fained to wend.° — *continue on*

39

"Perdy nay," said Malbecco, "shall ye not:
But let him pass as lightly, as he came:
For little good of him is to be got,[44]
And mickle° peril to be put to shame. — *much*
But let us go to seek my dearest dame,
Whom he hath left in yonder forest wild:
For of her safety in great doubt I am,
Lest savage beasts her person have despoiled:
Then all the world is lost, and we in vain have toiled."

40

They all agree, and forward them addressed:
"Ah but," said crafty Trompart, "weet ye well,
That yonder in that wasteful° wilderness — *wasteland*
Huge monsters haunt, and many dangers dwell;
Dragons, and minotaurs, and fiends of hell,
And many wild woodmen, which rob and rend
All travelers; therefore advise ye well,
Before ye enterprise that way to wend:
One may his journey bring too soon to evil end."

---

40. She's none of my business anymore.
41. In this case, *wonne* means "to dwell." Paridell suggests she wandered into the forest because she used to live there.
42. To slide off his saddle, perhaps to mend or adjust it.
43. When they realized Paridell wasn't staying to fight, Braggadocchio pretended to pursue him.
44. It's no good going after him.

41

Malbecco stopped in great astonishment,
And with pale eyes fast fixed on the rest,
Their counsel craved, in danger imminent.
Said Trompart, "You that are the most oppressed°   *heavy-laden*
With burden of great treasure, I think best
Here for to stay in safety behind;
My lord and I will search the wide forest."
That counsel pleased not Malbecco's mind;
For he was much afraid, himself alone to find.

42

"Then is it best," said he,° "that ye do leave   *Trompart*
Your treasure here in some security,
Either fast closed in some hollow grove,
Or buried in the ground from jeopardy,
Until we return again in safety:
As for us two, lest doubt of us ye have,
Hence far away we will blindfolded lie,
Nor privy be unto your treasure's grave."⁴⁵
It pleased: so he did, Then they march forward brave.

43

Now when amid the thickest woods they were,
They heard a noise of many bagpipes shrill,
And shrieking hubbubs them approaching near,
Which all the forest did with horror fill:
That dreadful sound the boaster's heart did thrill,°   *pierce*
With such amazement, that in haste he fled,
Nor ever looked back for good or ill,
And after him also fearful Trompart sped;
The old man could not flee, but fell to ground half dead.

44

Yet afterwards close creeping, as he might,
He in a bush did hide his fearful head,

---

45. In other words, "You may blindfold us before you hide your treasure, so that we won't know where it is."

The jolly satyrs full of fresh delight,
Came dancing forth, and with them nimbly led
Fair Hellenore, with garlands all bespread,
Whom their May-lady they had newly made:
She proud of that new honor, which they read,°   *realized*
And of their lovely° fellowship full glad,   *loving*
Danced lively, and her face did with a laurel shade.

45

The silly man that in the thicket lay
Saw all this goodly sport, and grieved sore,
Yet dared he not against it do or say,
But did his heart with bitter thoughts engore,°   *fill*
To see the unkindness of his Hellenore.[46]
All day they danced with great lustiness,
And with their horned feet the green grass wore,
The whiles their goats upon the brouzes° fed,   *new grasses*
Until drooping Phoebus began to hide his golden head.[47]

46

Though up they began their merry pipes to truss,°   *bundle*
And all their goodly herds did gather round,
But every satyr first did give a buss°   *kiss*
To Hellenore: so busses did abound.
Now began the humid vapor shed the ground
With pearly dew, and the earth's gloomy shade
Did dim the brightness of the welkin° round,   *sky*
That every bird and beast warned made,
To shroud themselves, whiles sleep their senses did invade.

47

Which when Malbecco saw, out of his bush
Upon his hands and feet he crept full light,
And like a goat amongst the goats did rush,
That through the help of his fair horns on height,[48]
And misty damp of misconceiving night,

---

46. But what of his own unkindness to her, when he kept her prisoner in an attempt to force her love?
47. Until the sun set.
48. A cuckold—a man whose wife had been unfaithful—was said to have been "given horns," as a goat.

And also through likeness of his goatish beard,
He did the better counterfeit aright:
So home he marched amongst the horned herd,
That none of all the satyrs him espied or heard.

48

At night, when all they went to sleep, he viewed,
Whereas his lovely wife amongst them lay,
Embraced of a satyr rough and rude,
Who all the night did mind his joyous play:
Nine times he heard him come aloft[49] ere day,
That all his heart with jealousies did swell;
But yet that night's example did betray,
That not for naught his wife them loved so well,
When one so oft a night did ring his matins bell.

49

So closely as he could, he to them crept,
When weary of their sport to sleep they fell,
And to his wife, that now full soundly slept,
He whispered in her ear, and did her tell,
That it was he, which by her side did dwell,
And therefore prayed her wake, to hear him plain.
As one out of a dream not waked well,
She turned her, and returned back again:
Yet her for to awake he did the more constrain.

50

At last with irksome trouble she abrayd;° *awakened*
And then perceiving, that it was indeed
Her old Malbecco, which did her upbraid,
With looseness of her love, and loathly deed,
She was astonished with exceeding dread,
And would have waked the satyr by her side;
But he her prayed, for mercy, or for meed,
To save his life, nor let him be descried,° *discovered*
But hearken to his lore, and all his counsel hide.

49. Arise, atop Hellenore.

51

Though began he her persuade, to leave that lewd
And loathsome life, of God and man abhorred,
And home return, where all should be renewed
With perfect peace, and bonds of fresh accord,
And she received again to bed and board,
As if no trespass° ever had been done: *sin*
But she it all refused at one word,
And by no means would to his will be won,
But chose amongst the jolly satyrs still to wonne.°   *abide*

52

He wooed her, until dayspring he espied;
But all in vain: and then turned to the herd,
Who butted him with horns on every side,
And trod down in the dirt, where his hoary° beard   *gray*
Was fouly dight,° and he of death afraid.   *befouled*
Early before the heavens' fairest light
Out of the ruddy east was fully reared,
The herds out of their folds were loosed quite,[50]
And he amongst the rest crept forth in sorry plight.

53

So soon as he the prison° door did pass,   *the goats' pens or barn*
He ran as fast, as both his feet could bear,
And never looked who behind him was,
Nor scarcely who before: like as a bear
That creeping close, amongst the hives to rear°   *lift*
An honeycomb, the wakeful dogs espy,
And him assailing, sore his carcass tear,
That hardly he with life away does fly,
Nor stays, till safe himself he see from jeopardy.[51]

54

Nor stayed he, till he came unto the place,
Where late his treasure he entombed had,
Where when he found it not (for Trompart base°   *lowly, dishonorably*

---

50. The goats were released from their pens.
51. Spenser is comparing Malbecco's escape to that of a bear who has been set upon by dogs.

Had it purloined for his master bad)
With extreme fury he became quite mad,
And ran away, ran with himself away:
That who so strangely had him seen bested,°   *tricked*
With upstart hair, and staring eyes dismay,
From Limbo lake him late escaped sure would say.[52]

55

High over hills and over dales he fled,
As if the wind him on his wings had borne,
Nor bank nor bush could stay him, when he sped
His nimble feet, as treading still on thorn:
Grief, and spite, and jealousy, and scorn
Did all the way him follow hard behind,
And he himself himself loathed so forlorn,
So shamefully forlorn of womankind,
That as a snake, still lurked in his wounded mind.

56

Still fled he forward, looking backward still,
Nor stayed his flight, nor fearful agony,
Until that he came unto a rocky hill,
Over the sea, suspended dreadfully,
That living creature it would terrify,
To look down, or upward to the height:
From thence he threw himself piteously,
All desperate of his fore-damned spirit,[53]
That seemed no help for him was left in living sight.

57

But through long anguish, and self-murdering thought
He was so wasted and forepined[54] quite,
That all his substance was consumed to naught,
And nothing left, but like an airy spirit,
That on the rocks he fell so flit and light,
That he thereby received no hurt at all,

---

52. Would think him a lost soul, indeed, who had been to the edge of Hell.
53. By fore-damned, Spenser is speaking of the belief that suicide is the only unforgiveable sin, since it throws away God's greatest gift to us: everything.
54. He was wasted away from pining for Hellenore and, therefore, not very heavy.

But chanced on a craggy cliff to light;°   *to land*
Whence he with crooked claws so long did crawl,
That at the last he found a cave with entrance small.

58

Into the same he creeps, and thenceforth there
Resolved to build his baleful mansion,
In dreary darkness, and continual fear
Of that rock's fall, which ever and anon
Threatens with huge ruin him to fall upon,
That he dare never sleep, but that one eye
Still open he keeps for that occasion;
Nor ever rests he in tranquility,
The roaring billows beat his bower so boisterously.

59

Nor ever is he wont on aught° to feed,   *anything*
But toads and frogs, his pasture poisonous,
Which in his cold complexion do breed
A filthy blood, or humor rancorous,
Matter of doubt and dread suspicious,
That doth with cureless care consume the heart,
Corrupts the stomach with gall vicious,
Crosscuts the liver with internal smart,
And doth transfix the soul with death's eternal dart.[55]

60

Yet can he never die, but dying lives,
And doth himself with sorrow new sustain,
That death and life at once unto him gives.
And painful pleasure turns to pleasing pain.
There dwells he ever, miserable swain,
Hateful both to himself, and every wight;
Where he through private grief, and horror vain,
Is waxed so deformed, that he has quite
Forgot he was a man, and Jealousy is hight.[56]

55. He was wasting away from within, both physically and spiritually.
56. He has become something of a beast ("claws") yet something of an immortal—jealousy in material form.

Word Play

Match the Spenserian words to their modern meanings.

aurora	*heal*
offend	*wound*
amend	*foolish*
fond	*the dawn*
wile	*songs*
board	*trick*
impeach	*table*
lays	*accuse*
scath	*raise*
rear	*penalty, harm*

Discussion Questions

1. How does Paridell win Hellenore's heart?

2. Remember, Spenser never strays far from his central theme, chastity. Does the tenth stanza mean that anyone can be "undone" by "continual battery"—by constant flattery and attention?

3. When Hellenore flees, she calls out for help. Is she pretending? Why or why not?

Canto XI.

Britomart chases Ollyphant,
finds Scudamour distressed:
Assails the house of Busyrane,
where Love's spoils are expressed.

1

O hateful hellish snake,[1] what fury first
Brought thee from baleful house of Proserpine,
Where in her bosom she thee long had nursed,
And fostered up with bitter milk of tine,°   *affliction*
Foul Jealousy, that turns love divine
To joyless dread, and makes the loving heart
With hateful thoughts to languish and to pine,
And feed itself with self-consuming smart?
Of all the passions in the mind thou vilest art.

2

O let him far be banished away,
And in his stead let Love forever dwell,
Sweet Love, that doth his golden wings embay°   *soak*
In blessed nectar, and pure pleasures well,
Untroubled of vile fear, or bitter fell.°   *woe*
And ye fair ladies, that your kingdoms make
In the hearts of men, them govern wisely well,
And of fair Britomart example take,
That was as true in love, as turtle to her mate.[2]

---

1. Spenser is speaking of Jealousy.
2. Well, not really. Spenser means the turtle *dove*, a symbol of faithfulness.

3

Who with Sir Satyrane, as earlier ye read,
Forth riding from Malbecco's hostless° house, — *inhospitable*
Far off espied a young man, the which fled
From an huge giant, that with hideous
And hateful outrage long him chased thus;
It was that Ollyphant, the brother dear
Of that Argante[3] vile and vicious,
From whom the Squire of Dames was reft whylere;° — *rescued from before*
This all as bad as she, and worse, if worse ought° were. — *anything*

4

For as the sister did in feminine
And filthy lust exceed all womankind,
So he surpassed his sex masculine,
In beastly use that I did ever find;
Whom when as Britomart beheld behind
The fearful boy so greedily pursue,
She was moved in her noble mind,
To employ her puissance to his rescue,
And pricked fiercely forward, where she him did view.

5

Nor was Sir Satyrane her far behind,
But with like fierceness did pursue the chase:
Whom when the giant saw, he soon rescinded
His former suit,[4] and from them fled apace;
They after both, and boldly bade him base,° — *issued a challenge*
And each did strive the other to outgo,° — *outrun*
But he them both outran a wondrous space,
For he was long, and swift as any roe,° — *deer*
And now made better speed, to escape his feared foe.

6

It was not Satyrane, whom he did fear,
But Britomart the flower of chastity;
For he the power of chaste hands might not bear,

---

3. The giantess defeated by Satyrane in Canto VII. Remember, she had flung aside the Squire of Dames for the fight.
4. The giant gave up on his original intention (catching the youth) and fled the knights.

But always did their dread encounter fly:
And now so fast his feet he did apply,
That he has gotten to a forest near,
Where he is shrouded in security.
The wood they enter, and search everywhere,
They searched diversely, so both divided were.

7

Fair Britomart so long him followed,
That she at last came to a fountain clear,
By which there lay a knight all wallowed
Upon the grassy ground, and by him near
His habergeon,° his helmet, and his spear;   *chain mail*
A little off, his shield was rudely thrown,
On which the winged boy° in colors clear   *Cupid*
Depicted was, full easy to be known,
And he thereby, where ever it in field was shown.

8

His face upon the ground did groveling lay,
As if he had been slumbering in the shade,
That the brave maid would not for courtesy,
Out of his quiet slumber him abrade,°   *awaken*
Nor seem too suddenly him to invade:
Still as she stood, she heard with grievous throb
Him groan, as if his heart were pieces made,
And with most painful pangs to sigh and sob,
That pity did the virgin's heart of patience rob.

9

At last forth breaking into bitter plaints°   *complaints, pleas*
He said, "O sovereign Lord that sits on high,
And reigns in bliss amongst thy blessed saints,
How suffers thou such shameful cruelty,
So long unwreaked° of thine enemy?   *unavenged*
Or hast thou, Lord, of good men's cause no heed?
Or doth thy justice sleep, and silent lie?
What booteth° then the good and righteous deed,   *use*
If goodness find no grace, nor righteousness no meed?°   *reward*

10

"If good find grace, and righteousness reward,
Why then is Amoret in captive band,
Since that more bounteous° creature never fared   *virtuous*
On foot, upon the face of living land?
Or if that heavenly justice may withstand
The wrongful outrage of unrighteous men,
Why then is Busyrane with wicked hand
Suffered, these seven months day in secret den
My lady and my love so cruelly to pen?

11

"My lady and my love is cruelly penned
In doleful darkness from the view of day,
Whilst deadly torments do her chaste breast rend,
And the sharp steel doth rive her heart in twain,
All for she Scudamour will not deny.[5]
Yet thou vile man, vile Scudamour art sound,
Nor can her aid, nor canst her foe dismay:°   *defeat*
Unworthy wretch to tread upon the ground,
For whom so fair a lady feels so sore a wound."[6]

12

There an huge heap of sobs did oppress
His struggling soul, and swelling throbs impeach
His faltering tongue with pangs of dreariness,
Choking the remnant of his plaintive speech,
As if his days were come to their last reach.
Which when she heard, and saw the ghastly fit,
Threatening into his life to make a breach,
Both with great ruth° and terror she was smote,   *pity*
Fearing lest from her cage the weary soul would flit.[7]

13

Though stooping down she him moved light,
Who therewith somewhat starting, up began look,

---

5. Essentially, Busyrane (an evil wizard) has taken Amoret captive and is tormenting her. Scudamour finds himself unable to rescue her and calls himself "vile" on account of it.
6. Though he loves her ("feels so sore a wound").
7. Scudamour's soul—souls were always referred to, like ships, as "she." *Flit* means "to flee."

And seeing him behind a stranger knight,
Whereas no living creature he mistook,
With great indignity he that sight forsook,[8]
And down again himself disdainfully
Abjectly, the earth with his fair forehead struck,
Which the bold virgin seeing, began apply
Fit medicine[9] to his grief, and spoke thus courteously.

14

"Ah gentle knight, whose deep conceived grief
Well seems to exceed the power of patience,
Yet if that heavenly grace some good relief
You send, submit you to high providence,
And ever in your noble heart prepense,°   *consider*
That all the sorrow in the world is less,
Than virtue's might, and value's confidence,
For who will not bide the burden of distress,
Must not here think to live: for life is wretchedness.

15

"Therefore, fair sir, do comfort to you take,
And freely read,° what wicked felon so   *reveal*
Hath outraged you, and enthralled your gentle mate.
Perhaps this hand may help to ease your woe,
And wreak your sorrow on your cruel foe,
At least it fair endeavour will apply."
Those feeling words so near the quick did go,[10]
That up his head he reared easily,
And leaning on his elbow, these few words let fly:

16

"What boots it plain,[11] that cannot be redressed,°   *repaired*
And sow vain sorrow in a fruitless° ear,[12]   *useless*
Since power of hand, nor skill of learned breast,

---

8. He looked away.
9. Remedy, not first aid.
10. In other words, her words hit close to home ("to the quick").
11. In other words, what use is it to complain, when there is no way to fix the problem?
12. Why tell you about my troubles ("sow sorrow") since you can't do anything?

Nor worldly price cannot redeem my dear,
Out of her thralldom and continual fear?
For he the tyrant, which her hath in ward
By strong enchantments and black magic lore,
Hath in a dungeon deep her closely barred,
And many dreadful fiends hath appointed to her guard.

17

"There he torments her most terribly,
And day and night afflicts with mortal pain,
Because to yield him love she doth deny,
Once to me yield, not to be yielded again:[13]
But yet by torture he would her constrain
Love to conceive in her disdainful breast;
Until so she do, she must in dolor° remain,   *sorrow*
Nor may by living means be thence released:
What boots it then to plain,° that cannot be redressed?"   *complain*

18

With this sad rehearsal of his heavy stress,
The warlike damsel was impassioned sore,
And said, "Sir knight, your cause is nothing less,
Than is your sorrow, certainly if not more;
For nothing so much pity doth implore,
As gentle lady's helpless misery.
But yet, if please ye listen to my lore,
I will with proof of last extremity,[14]
Deliver her from thence, or with her for you die."

19

"Ah gentlest knight alive," said Scudamour,
"What huge heroic magnanimity
Dwells in thy bounteous breast? What couldst thou more,
If she were thine,[15] and thou as now am I?
O spare thy happy days, and them apply

---

13. She would not abandon the love she bestowed upon Scudamour.
14. With greatest effort.
15. As if she were Britomart's own beloved.

To better boot,° but let me die, that ought;[16]　　　　　*uses*
More is more loss: one is enough to die."
"Life is not lost," said she, "for which is bought
Endless renown, that more than death is to be sought."

20

Thus she at length persuaded him to rise,
And with her wend,° to see what new success　　　　　*journey on*
Might him befall upon new enterprise;
His arms, which he had vowed to disprofess,°　　　　　*renounce*
She gathered up and did about him dress,
And his forwarded[17] steed unto him got:
So forth they both yfere° make their progress,　　　　　*together*
And march not past the maintenance of a shot,[18]
Until they arrived, whereas their purpose they did plot.

21

There they dismounting, drew their weapons bold
And stoutly came unto the castle gate;
Whereas no gate they found, them to withhold,
Nor warden to wait at morn and evening late,
But in the porch, that did them sore amaze,
A flaming fire, mixed with smoldering smoke,
And stinking sulfur, that with grisly hate
And dreadful horror did all entrance choke,
Enforced them their forward footing to revoke.[19]

22

Greatly thereat was Britomart dismayed,
Not in that astonishment wist,° how herself to bear;　　　　　*knew*
For danger vain it were, to have assailed
That cruel element, which all things fear,
Nor none can suffer to approach near:
And turning back to Scudamour, thus said,
"What monstrous enmity provoke we here,

---

16. In other words, don't bother yourself with my problems.
17. His horse had wandered off.
18. The distance of a bow-shot.
19. A wizard needs no gate or guard; his magic fire and smoke walled off his castle.

Foolhardy as the Earth's children, the which made
Battle against the gods? So we a god invade.

23

"Danger without discretion to attempt,
Inglorious and beastlike is:[20] therefore sir knight,
Aread° what course of you is safest deemed,   *reveal*
And how we with our foe may come to fight."
"This is," quoth he, "the dolorous spite,
Which earlier to you I complained: for neither may
This fire be quenched by any wit or might,
Nor yet by any means removed away,
So mighty be the enchantments, which the same do stay.

24

"What is there else, but cease these fruitless pains,
And leave me to my former languishing;
Fair Amoret must dwell in wicked chains,
And Scudamour here die with sorrowing."
"Perdy not so," said she, "for shameful thing
It were to abandon noble chivalry,
For show of peril, without venturing:
Rather let try extremities of chance,
Than enterprise° praise for dread to disadvance."°   *undertake / retreat*

25

Therewith resolved to prove her utmost might,
Her ample shield she threw before her face,
And her sword's point directing forward right,
Assailed the flame, the which soon gave place,°   *gave way*
And did itself divide with equal space,
That through she passed; as a thunder bolt[21]
Pierce the yielding air, and doth displace
The soaring clouds into sad showers melt;
So to her yielded the flames, and did their force revolt,°   *retreated*

---

20. Running into danger without a plan isn't very smart.
21. Get ready for another Spenserian epic simile. *Amplificatio,* remember?

26

Whom when Scudamour saw past the fire,
Safe and untouched, he likewise began assay,
With greedy will, and envious desire,
And bad the stubborn flames to yield him way:
But cruel Mulciber[22] would not obey
His threat-full pride, but did the more augment
His mighty rage, and with imperious sway
Him forced (maulgre)° his fierceness to relent, — *unwillingly*
And back retire, all scorched and pitifully burned.

27

With huge impatience he inwardly swelled,
More for great sorrow that he could not pass,
Than for the burning torment, which he felt,
That with fell woodness° he made fierce was, — *madness*
And willfully him throwing on the grass,
Did beat and bounce his head and breast full sore;
The whiles the championess now entered has
The outermost room, and past the foremost door,
The outermost room, abounding with all precious store.

28

For round about, the walls clothed were
With goodly arras° of great majesty, — *tapestries*
Woven with gold and silk so close and near,
That the rich metal lurked privily,
As faining to be hid from envious eye;
Yet here, and there, and everywhere unawares
It showed itself, and shone unwillingly;
Like a discolored snake, whose hidden snares° — *loops*
Through the green grass his long bright burnished back declares.

29

And in those tapestries were fashioned
Many fair portraits, and many a fair feat,
And all of love, and all of lustiness,

---

22. Another name for Vulcan, the god of fire.

As seemed by their semblance did entreat;°   *entice (the looker)*
And also all Cupid's wars they did repeat,
And cruel battles, which he whilome fought
Against all the gods, to make his empire great;
Besides the huge massacres, which he wrought
On mighty kings and Caesars, into thralldom brought.

30

Therein was writ,° how often thundering Jove   *depicted*
Had felt the point of his heart-piercing dart,
And leaving heaven's kingdom, here did rove
In strange disguise, to slake his scalding smart;[23]
Now like a ram, fair Helle to pervert,
Now like a bull, Europa to withdraw:
Ah, how the fearful lady's tender heart
Did lively seem to tremble, when she saw
The huge seas under her to obey her servant's law.[24]

31

Soon after that into a golden shower
Himself he changed fair Danaë to view,
And through the roof of her strong brazen tower
Did rain into her lap an honey dew,
The while her foolish guard, that little knew
Of such deceit, kept the iron door fast barred,
And watched, that none should enter nor issue;
Vain was the watch, and bootless° all the ward,°   *useless / prison*
When the god to golden hue himself transferred.

32

Then was he turned into a snowy swan,
To win fair Leda to his lovely trade:
O wondrous skill, and sweet wit of the man,

---

23. Jove pursued many lovers and took many different forms to do so. Here, Spenser recounts several of them. Then he'll recount myths about several other gods—stories already well-known to his readers. Explaining them all here, in detail, would take far too long and are basically irrelevant to the story. But I will hit some high points.

24. As is obvious, Jupiter turned into a ram, a bull, and a cow. In the last instance, he carried his beloved across the sea.

That her in daffodils sleeping made,
From scorching heat her dainty limbs to shade:
Whiles the proud bird ruffling his feathers wide,
And brushing his fair breast, did her invade;
She slept, yet twixt her eyelids closely spied,
How towards her he rushed, and smiled at his pride.

33

Then showed it, how the Thebane Semelee
Deceived of jealous Juno, did require
To see him in his sovereign majesty,
Armed with his thunderbolts and lightning fire,
Whence dearly she with death bought her desire.[25]
But fair Alcmena better match did make,
Enjoying his love in likeness more entire;
Three nights in one, they say, that for her sake
He then did put, her pleasures linger to partake.

34

Twice was he seen in soaring eagle's shape,
And with wide wings to beat the buxom° air,   *yielding*
Once, when he with Asterie did escape,
Again, when as the Trojan boy so fair[26]
He snatched from Ida hill, and with him bore:
Wondrous delight it was, there to behold,
How the rude shepherds after him did stare,
Trembling through fear, lest down he fallen should,
And often to him calling, to take surer hold.[27]

35

In satyr's shape Antiopa he snatched:
And like a fire, when he Aegin assayed:
A shepherd, when Mnemosyne he caught:
And like a serpent to the Thracian maid.
Whiles thus on earth great Jove these pageants played,

---

25. Semele wasn't sure if Jupiter was really a god so she asked to see him in his glory and—kerpoof!
26. This is Ganymede, later the cupbearer to the gods.
27. Hang on tight!

The winged boy did thrust into his throne,[28]
And scoffing, thus unto his mother said,
"Lo now the heavens obey to me alone,
And take me for their Jove, whiles Jove to earth is gone."

36

And thou, fair Phoebus, in thy colors bright
Was there woven, and the sad distress,
In which that boy thee plunged, for despite,
That thou betrayed his mother's wantonness,
When she with Mars was mingled in joyfulness:
Therefore, he thrilled thee with a leaden dart,
To love fair Daphne, which thee loved less:
Less she thee loved than was thy just dessert,
Yet was thy love her death, and her death was thy smart.[29]

37

So loved thou the lusty Hyacinth,
So loved thou the fair Coronis dear:
Yet both are of thy hapless hand extinct,[30]
Yet both in flowers do live, and love thee bear,
The one a pansy, the other a sweet briar:
For grief whereof, ye might have lively° seen   *quickly*
The god himself rending his golden hair,
And breaking quite his garland ever green,
With other signs of sorrow and impatient teene.°   *grief*

38

Both for those two, and for his own dear son,
The son of Climene[31] he did repent,
Who bold to guide the chariot of the Sun,
Himself in thousand pieces fondly rent,
And all the world with flashing fire burned;
So like, that all the walls did seem to flame.

---

28. In other words, Cupid attempted to take over while Jove was away.
29. That complicated myth about Apollo, a lover he lost, and finally Daphne, who fled from him and was turned into a laurel tree.
30. Killed at Phoebus Apollo's own command.
31. Spenser refers to Phaethon, who asked to drive his father's chariot (the sun).

Yet cruel Cupid, not herewith content,
Forced him soon to follow other game,
And love a shepherd's daughter for his dearest dame.

39

He loved Isse for his dearest dame,
And for her sake her cattle fed a while,
And for her sake a cowherd vile° became,   *lowly*
The servant of Admetus cowherd vile,
Whiles that from heaven he suffered exile.
Long were to tell each other lovely fit,°   *illness, lovesickness*
Now like a lion, hunting after spoil,
Now like a stag, now like a falcon flit:
All which in that fair arras was most lively writ.

40

Next unto him was Neptune pictured,
In his divine resemblance wondrous like:
His face was rugged, and his hoary head
Dropped with brackish dew; his three-forked pike°   *his trident*
He sternly shook, and therewith fierce did strike
The raging billows, that on every side
They trembling stood, and made a long broad dike,
That his swift chariot might have passage wide,
Which four great hippodames[32] did draw in team-wise tied.

41

His sea-horses did seem to sport amayne,°   *mightily*
And from their nostrils blow the briny stream,
That made the sparkling waves to smoke again,
And flame with gold, but the white foamy cream,
Did shine with silver, and shoot forth his beam.
The god himself did pensive seem and sad,
And hung down his head, as he did dream:
For privy love his breast empierced had,
Nor aught but dear Bisaltis ever could make him glad.

---

32. Seahorses; perhaps hippocampi (mythical beasts with the forepart of horses and scaly, coiling hindquarters).

42

He loved also Iphimedia dear,
And Aeolus' fair daughter Arne hight.
For whom he turned himself into a steer,
And fed on fodder, to beguile her sight.
Also to win Deucalion's daughter bright,
He turned himself into a dolphin fair;
And like a winged horse he took his flight,
To snaky-lock Medusa to repair,
On whom he got fair Pegasus, that flitteth in the air.

43

Next Saturn was, (but who would ever ween,
That sullen Saturn ever weened to love?
Yet love is sullen, and Saturn-like seen,
As he did for Erigone it prove)
That to a centaur did himself transmove.°   *transform*
So proved it also that gracious god of wine,
When for to encompass Philliras' hard love,
He turned himself into a fruitful vine,
And into her fair bosom made his grapes decline.

44

Long were to tell the amorous assays,
And gentle pangs, with which he[33] made meek
The mighty Mars, to learn his wanton plays:
How oft for Venus, and how often eke°   *also*
For many other nymphs he sore did shriek,°   *cry out for*
With womanish tears, and with unwarlike smarts,
Privily moistening his horrid° cheek.   *unshaven*
There was he painted full of burning darts,
And many wide wounds lanced through his inner parts.

45

Nor did he spare (so cruel was the elf)
His own dear mother, (ah why should he so?)
Nor did he spare sometime to prick himself,

---

33. Spenser means Cupid.

That he might taste the sweet consuming woe,[34]
Which he had wrought to many others more.
But to declare the mournful tragedies,
And spoils, wherewith he all the ground did strew,
More uneasy to number, with how many eyes
High heaven beholds sad lovers' nightly thieveries.°   *stealing of hearts*

46

Kings, queens, lords, ladies, knights, and damsels gentle
Were heaped together with the vulgar sort,
And mingled with the rascal rabblement,°   *rough crowds*
Without respect of person or of port,°   *importance*
To show Don[35] Cupid's power and great effort:
And round about a border was trailed,
Of broken bows and arrows shivered short,[36]
And a long bloody river through them railed,
So lively and so like that living sense it failed.[37]

47

And at the upper end of that fair room,
There was an altar built of precious stone,
Of passing value, and of great renown,
On which there stood an image[38] all alone,
Of massy gold, which with his own light shone;
And wings it had with sundry colors dight,
More sundry colors, then the proud pavone°   *peacock*
Bears in his boasted fan,° or Iris bright,   *fanned-out tail*
When her discolored bow she spreads through heaven's height.

48

Blindfold he was, and in his cruel fist
A mortal bow and arrows keen did hold,
With which he shot at random, when him list,[39]

---

34. He shot himself with his own arrows of love, that he might experience it.
35. "Don" (or "Dan") was a title of respect. As in, "Don Corleone."
36. Broken arrows.
37. In other words, the tapestries were very realistic.
38. A statue of Cupid stood in the middle of the room, atop an altar.
39. Cupid is often portrayed as blindfolded, because his arrows seem to be shot at random.

Some headed with sad lead, some with pure gold;
(Ah man beware, how thou those darts behold)
A wounded dragon under him did lie,
Whose hideous tail his left foot did enfold,
And with a shaft was shot through either eye,
That no man forth might draw, nor no man remedy.

49

And underneath his feet was written thus,
Unto the victor of the gods this be
And all the people in that ample house
Did to that image bow their humble knee,
And oft committed foul idolatry.
That wondrous sight fair Britomart amazed,
Nor seeing could her wonder satisfy,
But ever more and more upon it gazed,
The while the passing brightness her frail senses dazed.

50

Though as she backward cast her busy eye,
To search each secret of that goodly sted,°   *homestead*
Over the door thus written she did spy
Be bold. She oft and oft it over-read,
Yet could not find what sense it figured,
But what so were therein or writ or meant,
She was not a whit° thereby discouraged   *a bit*
From prosecuting of° her first intent,[40]   *pursuing, accomplishing*
But forward with bold steps into the next room went.

51

Much fairer than the former was that room,
And richlier by many parts arrayed:
For not with arras made in painful° loom,   *painstaking*
But with pure gold it all was overlaid,
Wrought with wild antickes,° which their follies played,   *grotesque figures*
In the rich metal, as they living were.
A thousand monstrous forms therein were made,

---

40. Finding the wizard and rescuing Amoret.

Such as false love doth oft upon him wear:
For love in thousand monstrous forms doth oft appear.

52

And all about, the glistening walls were hung
With warlike spoils, and with victorious preys,
Of mighty conquerors and captains strong,
Which were whilome captive in their days
To cruel love, and wrought their own decays:[41]
Their swords and spears were broke, and hauberks rent;
And their proud garlands of triumphant bays° *berries*
Trodden in dust with fury insolent,
To show the victors' might and merciless intent.

53

The warlike maid beholding earnestly
The goodly ordinance° of this rich place, *weaponry*
Did greatly wonder, nor could satisfy
Her greedy eyes with gazing a long space:
But more she marveled that no footings trace,
Nor wight appeared, but wasteful emptiness,[42]
And solemn silence over all that place.
Strange thing it seemed, that none was to possess
So rich purveyance, nor them keep° with carefulness. *guard*

54

And as she looked about, she did behold,
How over that same door was likewise writ,
Be bold, be bold, and everywhere *Be bold,*
That much she mused, yet could not construe it
By any riddling skill, or common wit.
At last she spied at that room's upper end,
Another iron door, on which was writ,
Be not too bold; whereto though she did bend° *turn*
Her earnest mind, yet wist not what it might intend.

---

41. They brought about their own demises.
42. She saw no footprints and saw no people.

55

Thus she there waited until eventide,
Yet living creature none she saw appear:
And now sad shadows began the world to hide,
From mortal view, and wrap in darkness drear;
Yet not could she doff her weary arms,° for fear   *armor and weapons*
Of secret danger, nor let sleep oppress
Her heavy eyes with nature's burden dear,
But drew herself aside in sureness,
And her well appointed weapons did about her dress.°   *arrange*

Match the Spenserian words to their modern meanings.

fell	*complaints, pleas*
roe	*repaired*
abrade	*useless*
plaints	*awaken*
dismay	*defeat*
ruth	*deer*
prepense	*pity*
redressed	*woe*
fruitless	*journey on*
wend	*consider*

1. In her search for the giant, who does Britomart find? What is his condition?

2. Britomart is able to pass through the enchanter's flames and smoke. Scudamour is driven back. What might explain this?

3. Inside the castle, many doors have written above them, "Be Bold." What might this mean? What about the last door?

Canto XII.

*The masque[1] of Cupid, and the enchanted
Chamber are displayed,
Whence Britomart redeems fair
Amoret, through charms decayed.*

1

Though when as cheerless night covered had
Fair heaven with an universal cloud,
That every wight dismayed with darkness sad,
In silence and in sleep themselves did shroud,
She heard a shrilling trumpet sound aloud,
Sign of near battle, or got° victory;   *won*
Naught therewith daunted° was her courage proud,   *lessened*
But rather stirred to cruel enmity,°   *hostility*
Expecting ever, when some foe she might descry.°   *see*

2

With that, an hideous storm of wind arose,
With dreadful thunder and lightning mixed,
And an earthquake, as if it straight would loosen
The world's foundations from his center fixed;
A direful stench of smoke and sulfur mixed
Ensued, whose noxiousness filled the fearful sted,°   *homestead*
From the fourth hour of night until the sixth;[2]
Yet the bold Britoness was naught ydred,°   *afraid*
Though much moved, but steadfast still persevered.

---

1. Think more about a masquerade than a mask. This was a popular form of entertainment in medieval times. This particular kind of masque involves something of a parade. It is filled with Spenserian symbolism. As each character emerges, think about what Spenser might be saying about his central theme, chastity.
2. From 10 p.m. until midnight.

3

All suddenly a stormy whirlwind blew
Throughout the house, that clapped every door,
With which that iron wicket open flew,[3]
As it with mighty levers had been tore:
And forth issued, as on the ready floor
Of some theater, a grave personage,
That in his hand a branch of laurel bore,
With comely behavior and countenance sage,°   *wise*
Clad in costly garments, fit for tragic stage.

4

Proceeding to the midst, he still did stand,
As if in mind he somewhat had to say,
And to the vulgar beckoning with his hand,
In sign of silence, as to hear a play,
By lively actions he began bewray
Some argument of matter passionate;[4]
Which done, he backed retired soft away,
And passing by, his name discovered,°   *revealed*
Ease, on his robe in golden letters ciphered.°   *written*

5

The noble maid, still standing all this viewed,
And marveled at his strange intentions;
With that a joyous fellowship issued
Of minstrels, making goodly merriment,
With wanton bards, and rhymers° impudent,   *poets*
All which together sung full cheerfully
A lay° of love's delight, with sweet consent: *song*
After whom marched a jolly company,
In manner of a masque, arranged orderly.

6

The while a most delicious harmony,
In full strange notes was sweetly heard to sound,

---

3. Spenser means the door that had been barred to Britomart earlier.
4. Though he spoke not, this well-dressed but somber person made a sign for Britomart to be silent, and then made other signs she didn't understand. We will learn he's beckoning to others.

That the rare sweetness of the melody
The feeble senses wholly did confound,
And the frail soul in deep delight nigh drowned.
And when it ceased, shrill trumpets loud did bray,
That their report did far away rebound,
And when they ceased, it began again to play,
The whiles the masquers marched forth in trim array.

7

The first was Fancy,[5] like a lovely boy,
Of rare aspect, and beauty without peer;
Matchable either to that imp° of Troy,   *young man*
Whom Jove did love, and chose his cup to bear,
Or that same dainty lad, which was so dear
To great Alcides, that when as he died,
He wailed womanlike with many a tear,
And every wood, and every valley wide
He filled with Hylas' name; the nymphs also Hylas cried.

8

His garment neither was of silk nor say,
But painted plumes, in goodly order dight,
Like as the sunburned Indians do array
Their tawny bodies, in their proudest plight:°   *condition*
As those same plumes, so seemed he vain and light,
That by his gait° might easily appear;   *bearing*
For still he fared as dancing in delight,
And in his hand a windy fan did bear,
That in the idle air he moved still here and there.

9

And him beside marched amorous Desire,
Who seemed of riper years, then the other swain,°   *young man*
Yet was that other swain this elder's sire,
And gave him being, common to them twain:[6]

---

5. Fancy symbolizes imagination.
6. What Spenser means is that Fancy (imagination, or perhaps a partly imaginary image of the person we love) produces Desire.

His garment was disguised very vain,°   *fantastically, elaborately*
And his embroidered bonnet sat awry;
Twixt both his hands few sparks he close did constrain,
Which still he blew, and kindled busily,
That soon they life conceived, and forth in flames did fly.

10

Next after him went Doubt, who was clad
In a discolored coat,° of strange disguise,   *many-colored coat*
That at his back a broad capuccio[7] had,
And sleeves dependant Albanese-wise:
He looked askew with his mistrustful eyes,
And nicely° trod, as thorns lay in his way,   *carefully*
Or that the floor to shrink he did avyse,[8]
And on a broken reed he still did stay[9]
His feeble steps, which shrunk, when hard thereon he lay.

11

With him went Danger, clothed in ragged weed,
Made of bear's skin, that him more dreadful made,
Yet his own face was dreadful, nor did need
Strange horror,[10] to deform his grisly shade;
A net in the one hand, and a rusty blade
In the other was, this Mischief, that Mishap;[11]
With the one his foes he threatened to invade,
With the other he his friends meant to enwrap:
For whom he could not kill, he practiced to entrap.

12

Next him was Fear, all armed from top to toe,
Yet thought himself not safe enough thereby,
But feared each shadow moving to and fro,
And his own arms when glittering he did spy,

---

7. A capuccio was a hooded cloak; it symbolizes secrecy and fraud.
8. He felt it best to stay bent toward the floor, to make as little of himself as possible.
9. He was leaning on a crutch ("reed").
10. I.e., a scary mask.
11. Spenser implies there are two kinds of danger: the mischief of others and bad luck.

Or clashing heard, he fast away did fly,[12]
As ashes pale of hue, and wing-heeled;
And evermore on danger fixed his eye,
Against whom he always bent a brazen shield,
Which his right hand unarmed fearfully did wield.

13

With him went Hope in rank, a handsome maid,
Of cheerful look and lovely to behold;
In silken samite° she was light arrayed,   *fancy silk*
And her fair locks were woven up in gold;
She always smiled, and in her hand did hold
An holy water sprinkler, dipped in dew,
With which she sprinkled favors manifold,
On whom she list, and did great liking show,
Great liking unto many, but true love to few.

14

And after them Dissemblance, and Suspect[13]
Marched in one rank, yet an unequal pair:
For she was gentle, and of mild aspect,
Courteous to all, and seeming debonair,
Goodly adorned, and exceeding fair:
Yet was that all but painted, and purloined,[14]
And her bright brows were decked with borrowed hair:
Her deeds were forged, and her words false coined,[15]
And always in her hand two clews° of silk she twined.   *rolls*

15

But he was foul, ill-favored, and grim,
Under his eyebrows looking still askance;[16]
And ever as Dissemblance laughed on him,
He lowered on her with dangerous eye glance,
Showing his nature in his countenance;

---

12. There's a bit of the Cowardly Lion here—afraid of his own roar.
13. "Dissembling" is disguising (or even lying), so is it any wonder Suspicion followed closely?
14. In other words, her fairness was all make-up.
15. She even stole the words from others (plagiarism).
16. Looking with suspicion on everyone.

His rolling eyes did never rest in place,
But walked each where, for fear of hid mischance,
Holding a lattice° still before his face,   *a covering like a veil*
Through which he still did peep, as forward he did pace.

16

Next him went Grief, and Fury matched yfere;°   *together*
Grief all in sable° sorrowfully clad,   *black*
Down hanging his dull head, with heavy cheer,
Yet inwardly being more, than seeming sad:
A pair of pincers in his hand he had,
With which he pinched people to the heart,
That from thenceforth a wretched life they lad,°   *lead*
In willful languor and consuming smart,
Dying each day with inward wounds of dolor's dart.

17

But Fury was full ill appareled
In rags, that naked nigh she did appear,
With ghastly looks and dreadful dreariness;
For from her back her garments she did tear,
And from her head oft rent her snarled hair:
In her right hand a firebrand she did toss
About her head, still roaming here and there;
As a dismayed deer in chase embost,°   *driven*
Forgetful of his safety, hath his right way lost.

18

After them went Displeasure and Pleasance,[17]
He looking lumpish and full sullen sad,
And hanging down his heavy countenance;
She cheerful fresh and full of joyance glad,
As if no sorrow she nor felt nor dread;
That evil matched pair they seemed to be:
An angry Wasp the one in a vial had
The other in hers an honey-lady Bee;
Thus marched these six couples forth in fair degree.°   *manner*

---

17. Here's an interesting pair—Displeasure and Pleasure.

19

After all these there marched a most fair dame,[18]
Led of two grisly villains, the one Despite,
The other called Cruelty by name:
She doleful lady, like a dreary spirit,
Called by strong charms out of eternal night,
Had death's own image figured in her face,
Full of sad signs, fearful to living sight;
Yet in that horror showed a seemly grace,
And with her feeble feet did move a comely° pace.   *graceful*

20

Her breast all naked, as net° ivory,   *purest*
Without adorn of gold or silver bright,
Wherewith the craftsman[19] wonts it beautify,
Of her due honor was despoiled quite,
And a wide wound therein (O rueful sight)
Entrenched deep with knife accursed keen,[20]
Yet freshly bleeding forth her fainting spirit,
(The work of cruel hand) was to be seen,
That dyed in sanguine red her skin all snowy clean.

21

At that wide orifice her trembling heart
Was drawn forth, and in silver basin laid,
Quite through transfixed with a deadly dart,
And in her blood yet steaming fresh embayed:°   *still soaked*
And those two villains, which her steps upstayed,°   *supported*
When her weak feet could scarcely her sustain,
And fading vital powers began to fade,
Her forward still with torture did constrain,
And evermore increased her consuming pain.

22

Next after her the winged god himself°   *Cupid*
Came riding on a lion ravenous,

---

18. This is Amoret, held captive in the castle.
19. Specifically, craftsmen who make jewelry. They would wish to beautify her with their work.
20. She suffers a knife-wound, and her heart has been removed.

Taught to obey the ménage° of that Elf, *training*
That man and beast with power imperious
Subdued to his kingdom tyrannous:
His blindfold eyes he bade a while unbind,
That his proud spoil of that same dolorous
Fair dame he might behold in perfect kind;[21]
Which seen, he much rejoiced in his cruel mind.

23

Of which full proud, himself up rearing high,
He looked round about with stern disdain;
And did survey his goodly company:
And marshalling the evil-ordered train,[22]
With that the darts which his right hand did strain,
Full dreadfully he shook that all did quake,
And clapped on high his colored wings twain,
That all his many it afraid did make:
Though blinding him again,[23] his way he forth did take.

24

Behind him was Reproach, Repentance, Shame;
Reproach the first, Shame next, Repent behind:
Repentance feeble, sorrowful, and lame:
Reproach despiteful, careless, and unkind;
Shame most ill favored, bestial, and blind.
Shame lowered, Repentance sighed, Reproach did scold;
Reproach sharp stings, Repentance whips entwined,
Shame burning brand-irons[24] in her hand did hold:
All three to each unlike, yet all made in one mould.

25

And after them a rude confused rout
Of persons flocked, whose names were hard to read:
Amongst them was stern Strife, and Anger stout,
Unquiet Care, and fond Unthriftiness,

21. That he might see her clearly.
22. An eviltrain of characters.
23. Replacing his blindfold.
24. Probably swords.

Lewd Loss of Time, and Sorrow seeming dead,
Inconstant Change, and false Disloyalty,
Consuming Riotous, and guilty Dread
Of heavenly vengeance, faint Infirmity,
Vile Poverty, and lastly Death with infamy.

26

There were full many more like maladies,
Whose names and natures I could not read well;
So many more, as there be fantasies
In wavering women's wit, that none can tell,
Or pains in love, or punishments in hell;
All which disguised marched in masquing ways,
About the chamber with that damsel,
And then returned, having marched thrice,
Into the inner room, from whence they first did rise.[25]

27

So soon as they were in, the door straight way
Fast locked, driven with that stormy blast,
Which first it opened; and bore all away.
Then the brave maid, which all this while was placed,
In secret shade,[26] and saw both first and last,
Issued forth, and went unto the door,
To enter in, but found it locked fast:°   *firmly*
It vain she thought with rigorous uproar
For to force, when charms had closed it afore.

28

Where force might not avail, their sleights and art
She cast to use, both fit for hard enterprise;
For they, from that same room not to depart
Until morrow next, she did herself advise,
When that same masque again should forth arise.
The morrow next appeared with joyous cheer,
Calling men to their daily exercise,

---

25. They returned to the room from whence they came.
26. From a hiding place.

Then she, as morrow fresh, herself did rear
Out of her secret stand, that day for to outwear.²⁷

29

All that day she outwore in wandering,
And gazing on that chamber's ornament,
Until that again the second evening
Her covered with her sable vestment,
Wherewith the world's fair beauty she hath blent:°   *covered with a cloak*
Then when the second watch was almost past,
That brazen door flew open, and in went
Bold Britomart, as she had late forecast,°   *planned*
Neither of idle shows, nor of false charms aghast.°   *afraid*

30

So soon as she was entered, round about
She cast her eyes, to see what was become
Of all those persons, which she saw without:
But lo, they straight were vanished all and some,°   *all of them*
Nor living wight she saw in all that room,
Save that same woeful lady,° both whose hands   *Amoret*
Were bounden fast, that did her ill become,
And her small waist girt° round with iron bands,   *wrapped tightly*
Unto a brazen pillar, by the which she stands.

31

And her before the vile enchanter° sat,   *Busyrane*
Figuring° strange characters of his art,   *writing*
With living blood he those characters wrote,
Dreadfully dropping from her dying heart,²⁸
Seeming transfixed with a cruel dart,
And all perforce to make her him to love.
Ah who can love the worker of her smart?°   *he who caused her pain*
A thousand charms he formerly did prove;°   *try*
Yet thousand charms could not her stedfast heart remove.

---

27. In other words, she would wait throughout the day until that night's masque.
28. Busyrane (Spenser also spells it "Busirane") writes with a pen dipped in Amoret's blood.

32

Soon as that virgin knight he saw in place,
His wicked books in haste he overthrew,
Not caring his long labors to deface,°   *ruin*
And fiercely running to that lady° true,   *Amoret*
A murderous knife out of his pocket drew,
The which he thought, for villainous despite,
In her tormented body to imbrue:°   *embed*
But the stout damsel to him leaping light,
His cursed hand withheld, and mastered his might.

33

From her, to whom his fury first he meant,[29]
The wicked weapon rashly he did wrest,
And turning to herself his fell intent,
Unawares it struck into her snowy chest,
That little drops empurpled her fair breast.
Exceeding wroth therewith the virgin grew,
Although the wound were nothing deep pressed
And fiercely forth her mortal blade she drew,
To give him the reward for such vile outrage due.

34

So mightily she smote him, that to ground
He fell half dead; next stroke him should have slain,
Had not the lady,° which by him stood bound,   *Amoret*
Dernely° unto her called to abstain,   *earnestly*
From doing him to die. For else her pain
Should be remediless, since none but he,
Which wrought it, could the same cure again.
Therewith she stayed her hand, loath stayed to be;
For life she him envied,° and longed revenge to see.   *sought to take from him*

35

And to him said, "Thou wicked man, whose meed°   *just reward*
For so huge mischief, and vile villainy
Is death, or if that ought do death exceed,

---

29. Busyrane rushes at Britomart with a knife and strikes her a glancing blow to the chest.

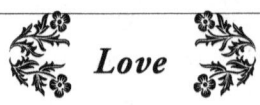 **Love**

Although Book III of *The Faerie Queene* is about chastity, it touches on the subject of love, as well. What does the Bible have to say about love? Quite a bit, actually. Here, it's shown to be not a state of being—as in, "She's in love"—but instead a consistent, conscious attitude, and a series of actions.

> Love is patient, love is kind. It does not envy, it does not boast, it is not proud. It does not dishonor others, it is not self-seeking, it is not easily angered, it keeps no record of wrongs. Love does not delight in evil but rejoices with the truth. It always protects, always trusts, always hopes, always perseveres. Love never fails. (1 Cor. 13:4–8a)

So far, we've seen few examples in Spenser's saga of love that live up to this high ideal. Britomart fell in love with an image; in Canto XII, we see (in the two endings) the dual nature of the relationship between Amoret and Scudamore. Prince Arthur's love for the Faerie Queene (Glorianna) is selfless and fits most of this description; perhaps that is the ideal that Spenser, had he finished his masterpiece, would have shown us.

Be sure, that naught may save thee from to die,
But if that thou this dame do presently
Restore unto her health, and former state;
This do and live, else die undoubtedly."
He glad of life, that looked for° death but late,   *expected*
Did yield himself right willing to prolong his date.

36

And rising up, began straight to overlook,
Those cursed leaves,° his charms back to reverse;   *pages*
Full dreadful things out of that baleful book
He read, and measured many a sad verse,
That° horror began the virgin's heart to pierce,   *resulting that*
And her fair locks up stared stiff on end,
Hearing him those same bloody lines rehearse;°   *say*
And all the while he read, she did extend
Her sword high over him, if ought he did offend.

37

Anon she began perceive the house to quake,
And all the doors to rattle round about;
Yet all that did not her dismayed make,
Nor slacken her threat-full hand for dangers doubt,°   *feared*
But still with steadfast eye and courage stout
Abode, to weet what end would come of all.
At last that mighty chain, which round about
Her tender waist was wound, down began fall,
And that great brazen pillar broke in pieces small.

38

The cruel steel, which thrilled° her dying heart,   *pierced*
Fell softly forth, as of his own accord,
And the wide wound, which lately did part
Her bleeding breast, and riven bowels gored,
Was closed up, as it had not been bored,[30]
And every part to safety full sound,
As she were never hurt, was soon restored:
Though when she felt herself to be unbound,
And perfect whole, prostrate she fell unto the ground.

39

Before fair Britomart, she fell prostrate,
Saying, "Ah noble knight, what worthy meed
Can wretched lady, quit° from woeful state,   *rescued*
Yield you in lieu of this your gracious deed?
Your virtue self her own reward shall breed,
Even immortal praise, and glory wide,
Which I your vassal, by your prowess freed,
Shall through the world make to be notified,
And goodly well advance, that goodly well was tried."[31]

40

But Britomart upraising her from ground,
Said, "Gentle dame, reward enough I ween

---

30. As if it had never been pierced (bored into).
31. She means she will spread the news of Britomart's deed and her glory, which was proven ("tried") by that act.

For many labors more, then I have found,
This, that in safety now I have you seen,
And means of your deliverance have been:
Henceforth fair lady comfort to you take,
And put away remembrance of late teen;°   *wound*
Instead thereof know, that your loving mate,
Hath no less grief endured for your gentle sake."³²

41

She much was cheered to hear him mentioned,
Whom of all living wights she loved best.
Then laid the noble championess strong hand
Upon the enchanter, which had her distressed
So sore, and with foul outrages oppressed:
With that great chain, wherewith not long ago
He bound that piteous lady prisoner, now released,
Himself she bound, more worthy to be so,
And captive with her led to wretchedness and woe.³³

42

Returning back, those goodly rooms, which earlier
She saw so rich and royally arrayed,
Now vanished utterly, and clean subversed°   *upset*
She found, and all their glory quite decayed,
That sight of such a change her much dismayed.
Thence forth descending to that perilous porch,
Those dreadful flames she also found delayed,°   *gone*
And quenched quite, like a consumed torch,
That earlier all enterers wont so cruelly to scorch.

43

More easy issue° now, than entrance late   *exit*
She found: for now that feigned dreadful flame,
Which choked the porch of that enchanted gate,
And passage barred to all, that thither came,

---

32. Scudamour suffered no less than Britomart for Amoret's sake.
33. Britomart bound the wizard in order to bring him to justice (presumably at the Faerie Queene's court).

Was vanished quite, as it were not the same,
And gave her leave at pleasure forth to pass.
The enchanter self, which all that fraud did frame,
To have forced the love of that fair lass,
Seeing his work now wasted deep aggrieved was.

44

But when the victoress arrived there,
Where late she left the pensive Scudamour,
With her own trusty squire, both full of fear,
Neither of them she found where she them lore:°   *left*
Thereat her noble heart was astonished sore;
But most fair Amoret, whose gentle spirit
Now began to feed on hope, which she before
Conceived had, to see her own dear knight,
Being thereof beguiled was filled with new fright.

45

But he, sad man, when he had long in dread
Awaited there for Britomart's return,
Yet saw her not nor sign of her good speed,
His expectation to despair did turn,
Misdeeming° sure that her those flames did burn;   *mistaking*
And therefore began advise with her old squire,
Who her dear nursling's° loss no less did mourn,   *the one she had nursed*
Thence to depart for further aide to inquire:
Where let them wend at will, whilest here I do respire.[34]

---

34. Spenser allows the women to go on their way (wend at will), while he rests, exhausted from his labors. The 1590 edition had quite a different, happier ending. In its final verses, Scudamour has not left the scene, and a loving reunion occurs between him and Amoret. Britomart, however, envies them and wishes to find her own true love and finally to end her quest. The change to this darker ending was made in the 1596 edition. I have chosen to use this darker one, instead, because it was Spenser's later intention.

Word Play

Match the Spenserian words to their modern meanings.

masque	*graceful*
daunted	*a dance, procession*
sage	*written*
ciphered	*black*
imp	*lessened*
swain	*young man (1)*
samite	*wise*
sable	*young man (2)*
embost	*fancy silk*
comely	*driven*

Discussion Questions

1. We're focused on chastity here. Explain what role in chastity these characters play: Fancy (fantasy), Desire, Doubt, Danger, Fear, Hope, Dissemblance, Suspicion, Grief, Fury, Displeasure, Pleasure, Despite, and Cruelty.

2. Why do the maladies (beginning with Reproach and ending with Death) follow at Cupid's call?

3. Why might Spenser have changed the ending of this book in his second edition?

www.ingramcontent.com/pod-product-compliance
Lightning Source LLC
Chambersburg PA
CBHW071001160426
43193CB00012B/1862